# COLUMBUS

# Debunking of a Legend

# COLUMBUS
## Debunking
### of a
## Legend

by
Vincent Sinovcic

RIVERCROSS PUBLISHING, INC.
NEW YORK

First Edition

ISBN: 0-944957-06-4

Library of Congress Catalog Card Number: 90-8418

Sinovcic, Vincent, 1933-
    Columbus, debunking of a legend / by Vincent Sinovcic.—1st ed.
    p.  cm.
    Includes bibliographical references.
    ISBN 0-944957-06-4 : $14.95
    1. Columbus, Christopher. 2. America—Discovery and exploration—Spanish. I. Title.
E111.S54 1990
970.01′5—dc20                                                    90-8418
                                                                    CIP

*SSH*

# CONTENTS

# DEDICATION

To the anonymous, heroic and tragic crew of the caravel
ATLANTE which, in 1484, found America

# COLUMBUS

## Debunking of a Legend

# PART I.

## The Enigma of Christopher Columbus

There is a notion largely accepted today that Christopher Columbus, the official discoverer of America, was an Italian born
in Genoa whose original name was Christoforo Colombo. This
notion generally prevailed in Columbus' own time, too. Most
of the sources mention him as being from Genoa or some place
near Genoa on the Ligurian Coast.

Apparently, numerous families named Colombo lived in 15th
century Genoa and Italian researchers and historical institutions
patronized and financed by the City of Genoa and Italian government have found and brought forward a number of Genoese
and other documents pertinent to certain Christoforo Colombo
and his family. Those documents (over 200 of them) were put
together in collection called the Raccolta Colombiana edited and
published for the first time in 1892, by Cesare Lollis in connection
with Genoa exposition celebrating the 400th anniversary of the
discovery. Many of these documents were republished since on
several occasions.

On the basis of those papers, the family background and the
early life of the official discoverer of America was reconstructed
(approximately) as follows:

Christopher Columbus was born as Christoforo Colombo in
Genoa in 1451, somewhere between August and October of that
year. His father Domenico Colombo was a wool-weaver by
profession, his mother Susanna Fontanarossa was a daughter
of a peasant and also wool-weaver from Bisagno, apparently
well provided. The family Colombo can be traced in Genoa back
to Christopher's grandfather Giovanni, also a wool-weaver.

Christoforo had a younger brother, Bartolomeo, born in 1462, and one much younger, Giacomo, born in 1468. He also had one more brother, Giovanni Pellegrino, and a sister of whom nothing much is known.

Christoforo went to sea when he was 14-years old, according to some reports, probably for some occasional trip only—most of the time he was helping his father in his wool-weaving business. His name is first mentioned in the notorial records of Genoa together with his father when the Colombos were involved in a lawsuit against one Girolamo del Porto. The same Christoforo is mentioned again that year in another notorial record where he is described as being over 19 years of age. By 1470, his family moved from Genoa and settled in Savona where his father bought a tavern while still practicing his wool-weaving business. The young Christoforo was there too, helping his father and working as a woolworker. His presence in Savona is attested by three notorial records in 1472–1473, in which Christoforo was described as "woolmaker from Genoa". In 1474–1475, he probably made one or two trips as a sailor on Genoese ships to the Island of Chios. In 1476, he sailed with the Genoese merchant fleet carrying valuable cargo to Flanders. But, the Genoese fleet was attacked by French pirates, by the famous French corsair-admiral Guillome de Casanove Coullon near Cape of St. Vincent, thirty-six leagues from Cadiz. In the ensuing battle, the ship on which Columbus navigated burned and sank, but being a strong swimmer, though wounded, he managed to hold onto an oar which helped him to stay afloat, and he swam to the safety of the Portuguese shore. He then reached Lisbon where his younger brother Bartolomeo, according to some sources, was already living, and was helped by other Genoese also living there in a large Genoese colony. The following year Columbus again embarked as a seaman on Genoese ships on their voyage to Bristol in England and North to Iceland. In 1478, Columbus was sent by Paolo di Negro to Madeira to buy sugar and, in 1479, he married in Lisbon one Felipa Perestrello e Moniz, a young Portuguese who was, surprisingly, from distinguished noble family. In 1480, he moved to the house of his mother-in-law on the Island of Porto Santo (near Madeira). In 1482–1484, maybe, he took part in a Portuguese voyage to Guinea. Soon after, he proposed to John II, the King of Portugal a "revolutionary" project of reaching India by sailing West and crossing the Atlantic. But the project was rejected by the Crown of Portugal, and Columbus, disappointed, decided to leave the country and offer his plans to someone else. Near the end of 1485, he settled in Spain—permanently. From now on his history is very well known.

This is the usual line on the early life of Columbus which, with some minor rectifications here and there, is generally propagated and largely accepted today.

* * * * *

Reconstructed in this way the story of the early life of the great mariner seems all clear and simple. Yet, the story is not complete nor certain. The questions remain despite the numerous papers which are presented as supposed evidence and despite the support of powerful international interests which are anxious, even today, to preserve the traditional notion of Columbus as being both a genuine Genoese and a genuine discoverer of the New World. For, strange as it may look, the question of ethnical background of Columbus and even more of his role in the discovery is not just an academic question left for historians to debate. It still has, today, profound political implications. [1]But, political considerations aside, it must be immediately pointed out that there are also other data, declarations and testimonies, including some from Columbus himself, to dispute and contradict the Genoese evidence. In fact, almost everything we know about him tends to leave a long shadow over the well-established notion of Columbus as Genoese. The other data show the other Columbus diametrically opposed and different and thus very difficult to identify with the woolmaker from Genoa . . .

The first difficulty in identification of Columbus the Discoverer with Christoforo Colombo the Genoese woolmaker is presented by the question of the age of Columbus. The disparity in age seems obvious, the comparison does not fit. The Genoese documents show that Chistoforo Colombo was born in 1451. This is proven beyond doubt by two documents which mention his age in precise words. The question is only in couple of months (between August 26th and October 31st in 1451). This means that Columbus was only 34 years old when he came to Spain, was only 41 when he went to the voyage of discovery, and died at the age of 54, in Valladolid.

However, this does not correspond well with the facts we know about Columbus; neither is it in accord with some of his own declarations:

1.) When the totally gray Columbus came to Spain in 1485, he was obviously an older man (older than 34). All his Spanish contemporaries shared that impression. In fact, in Spain, some referred to Columbus as "El Viejo"—the Old One.

2.) On December 21st 1492, Columbus wrote in his diary that he has been navigating at sea for twenty-three years continuously without leaving the sea for any time worth counting. [2] His son Fernando said that his father went to sea when he was 14 years old. If this is so then Columbus began to navigate several years before 1465. He then must have been older at least by a few years.

3.) A similar conclusion follows from Columbus' letter dated in 1501, in which he said he had been navigating for "over forty years". Since he was away from the sea for more than ten years this means Columbus began to navigate roughly in 1451, the year the Genoese Colombo was born. That would fix Columbus' date of birth circa 1436, and would prove that he died at the age of about seventy as it has been reported by one reliable source. Even if Columbus counted those ten or more years when he was away from the sea as actual navigation, as it is suggested by some authors, this still would make him at least four to five years older than the woolmaker from Genoa.

4.) Also in his famous letter from Jamaica dated July 7, 1503, Columbus himself hints clearly at his old age. This is what he says to himself: "Turn to Him (God) and recognize your error at last. His mercy is without limit. Your age will not impede great things. He has the greatest mansions. Abraham was over hundred years old when he fathered Isaac and Sarah too was no more a young girl".[3] This is an old and tired man speaking, not the one who, normally, would be at 51, still in possession of all his forces. It is truly an old man's lament, and the self-consoling mention of Abraham, "over hundred years old", gives it an added significance. Columbus must had been then closer to his seventies than to his fifties.

5.)   That Columbus the Discoverer was older than the wool-maker from Genoa is also indicated by another statement of Columbus, the one that he was once in service of King René of Anjou, the French pretender to the thrones of Naples and Aragon. Columbus, if we are to believe him, was the captain of a vessel of King René and was entrusted the mission by this Prince to capture the galleass Fernandina from the King of Aragon. The Historians are amused by this contention of Columbus. Most of them, however, accept it as genuine. They agree that this episode in the life of Christoforo Colombo, Genoese, historically, could have happened only in 1472–1473. But, this is excluded and is impossible for three following reasons: First, Christoforo Colombo was not the naval officer then. He was working as a woolweaver as the same Genoese documents attest. Besides, the alleged captain was then only 21 years old! Second, it is impossible because René of Anjou was a notorious enemy of Genoa and third, it is impossible because as the same Genoese notorial records show, Christoforo Colombo, in 1472–1473, was home in Savona on Genoese territory helping his father in his wool-weaving business. In March of 1472, Christoforo Colombo, described as a "woolmaker from Genoa" witnessed a will in Savona in company with certain tailor named Domenico Vigna. He is again mentioned in Savona in August of 1472, and again in August of the following year.[4] Therefore, if Columbus was ever in the service of René of Anjou this could had been only some-time around 1460, when this Prince fought with Ferrante, the illegitimate son of Alfonso V of Aragon for the possession of the Kingdom of Naples as some authors have observed. This points out again that Columbus was born somewhere between 1430 and 1440.

Even if this episode never happened, if it was not true, same as his "over forty years" of navigation were certainly not true, the fact that he insisted on it anyway shows that he was in reality an older man. He surely was smart enough not to insist on something which would be in conflict with his actually much younger age.

6.)   In 1505, Columbus was so old and weak that he was obliged to seek the royal licence (which was needed by the law) to ride a mule because he was not in condition to ride a horse. His son Diego obtained this licence for his father on account of both ill health and old age. The word used was "ancianidad" which in Spanish has the strict meaning and applies to those who are very old. Certainly the Admiral was around seventy. He may have been easily past seventy.

7.)   Andres Bernaldez, the contemporary chronicler of Spain noted the death of Columbus in 1506, in Valladolid, and said of him "he was 70 years old, more or less."

The testimony of Bernaldez as a historical source is very important. Bernaldez was not a mere contemporary; he personally knew Columbus, was his friend and host and certainly had enough opportunity to inform himself about the approximate age of the Admiral.

All said, the testimonies about the age of the Discoverer differ from the data pertinent to Christoforo Colombo the woolmaker from Genoa. This cannot be denied. Even a number of pro-Genoese historians recognize this fact and many are pushing his birthdate further back, usually citing 1446 or 1447, as the most likely year, without, however, explaining what to make out of those Genoese documents which say that he was born in 1451 . . !

Furthermore, even the data on his brothers are uncertain, which complicates the issue twice as much. There are no clear-cut testimonies relative to the age of Bartolome and Diego the two brothers of the Admiral, but there are strong indications that they both also must have been older than those Genoese documents show.

The age of Bartolome is stated in 1512, during the lawsuit between his nephew and the Crown of Spain. In this Bartolome declared himself to be "fifty years old, or more". Fifty years would have been the exact age of Bartolomeo Colombo for whom it was said that he was born in 1462. However the confusion was created by Bartolome himself adding "or more". Men, same as women, do not give themselves more years than they really have. How much more?

According to some sources when Colombus reached Lisbon

in 1476, his brother Bartolome had already been there for a year. If this is so he must have been definitively older too, for it is difficult to believe that he established himself alone in a faraway country at the tender age of thirteen.

As for the age of Diego, the youngest one, there is a line on him in one letter written to King Ferdinand in 1512. In it Diego is described as "old, poor and sick." Since it is hardly believable that a man of only forty-four would be described as old, it follows that he too was probably older than those Genoese documents show. There is even a possibility that Diego was actually the oldest of the three Columbus brothers. Diego was a "man of the church" (a monk). Some point out that in those times it was a custom to give a first born to the church. Furthermore, that obscure woolweaver found in some Genoese papers named Domenico Colombo, whom the pro-Genoese historians insist was his father, lived to a ripe old age and died in his 80's, while no one of his alleged sons ever reached old age which is somewhat strange. If they were the Colombos from Genoa then Christopher died at age of 54, Bartolome at 52, while the "old" Diego died when he was only 47-years old! Even, genetically speaking, not too convincing!

In summary the data on the age of Columbus and his brothers do not fit well with those known from the Colombos who were the woolworkers from Genoa.

\* \* \* \* \*

Another difficulty in the identification of Columbus with the Genoese Colombo is presented by the apparent nobility of Columbus. There are abundant indications of his aristocratic origin which are totally incompatible with the publican family of Colombos the Genoese woolweavers. Columbus himself insisted in being a genuine nobleman. This cannot be dismissed lightly as some pro-Genoese authors do by declaring it to be untrue and a product of his imagination and vanity, or by some others who simply ignore it without any comment. Nevertheless the indications are overwhelming. How else can the fact be explained that the two Columbus brothers are found always involved with the aristocracy? Christopher Columbus, though allegedly a Genoese plebeian, former wool-weaver turned simple seaman, foreigner and penniless, circulates exclusively among the nobility, marries into nobility, associates, argues and bargains with counts, dukes, kings and their ministers. Christopher, described as a "gracious," "eloquent" gentleman, "puffed with pride," was accepted everywhere as a genuine nobleman and so was his brother Bartolome.

This was well known at the Court of Spain. In 1493, Columbus' coat-of-arms was enlarged; he was granted the privilege by the King and Queen of Spain—a rare honor very doubtful to be conferred upon a commoner—to add to his personal family blazon the royal arms of Castile and Leon, "preserving the base of it for your own arms, those that You are accustomed to wear." The one he wore—his original and personal coat-of-arms is known: a blue band on a gold field with a red chief.

Even before his arrival in Spain when he resided in Portugal, Columbus was known there too as a man of noble birth. His marriage, for one, attests to it: He married an aristocratic Portuguese girl named Felipa Perestrello e Moniz who was both young and beautiful. Felipa was of noble lineage from both sides of her family. Her father Bartholomeu Perestrello descended from one noble Italian family originally from Piacenza which settled in Portugal. In 1446, he was named by Prince Henry the Navigator the hereditary captain of the Island of Porto Santo near Madeira. On her mother's side she descended from one of the oldest families of Portugal linked with almost all the leading families in the country. Her mother Isabel Moniz was a cousin of the ducal House of Braganças; that is to say she was a relative of the Portuguese royal family! How it came about that a poor Genoese seaman and plebeian married a girl of such lineage is one of many unresolved questions concerning Christopher Columbus. The explanation of pro-Genoese historians is simple: Isabel Moniz was a widow and poor and she was just happy to marry Felipa to anyone to get rid of her. But, this simply is not true. Her late husband was a hereditary captain of the Island of Porto Santo and after his death the captaincy was inherited by his widow. She later resigned it and gave it to her nephew, which means she was economically so well of that the captaincy of the island was of no particular importance for her. Furthermore, Dona Isabel was wealthy enough to keep Felipa in an exclusive convent and boarding school for noble girls in faraway Lisbon, and Columbus himself, after his marriage went to Porto Santo to live in the house of his mother-in-law where he spent over five years doing nothing, and where his older son Diego was born. It follows, at that time, Felipa was not so poor after all.[5] (Isabel Moniz also owned a house in Funchal on Madeira in which Columbus lived for most of the time).

The nobility of Columbus was no doubt well known and believed at the Court of Portugal. In any case, the Court considered him unquestionably as such as it is shown from the royal letter of March 1488, when Columbus, after his initial disappointment in Spain, decided to return to Portugal and wrote about it to the Court of Lisbon. King John II answered Columbus in a letter which is very significant in regard to the noble background of Columbus. In it the King treats him almost as his equal. He calls him "our special friend" and not only guarantees him the safe conduct and freedom of any possible persecution, but heaps praises on him; the King excuses himself for any inconvenience Columbus may have endured previously in Portugal, he almost begs him to return and promises to arrange all the things as to please him! The letter was addressed: "To Christouon Collon our special friend in Seville".[6]

Once, some just did not believe in this letter which the King sent to "his special friend" precisely because of it style and content, but the letter is proven to be authentic whose original still exists today in the archives of Columbus family, the Dukes of Veragua.[7] That much for Columbus' noble ancestry. (On the strength of this letter one Portuguese historian constructed a hypothesis that Columbus in reality was one Portuguese aristocrat and cousin of the King John II!) Another Portuguese historian believes that Columbus was a nephew of King John II.

* * * * *

Further difficulty in identifying Christopher Columbus and his brothers with the Genoese woolworkers is posed by the question about the education of the Admiral, for Christopher Columbus shows all the signs of a man who undoubtedly received a fairly good schooling. He possessed a vast knowledge of scientific as well as humanistic matters. In other words we may say Columbus received one regular education which a nobleman of his time was generally supposed to have. He knew grammar well which enabled him to learn other languages; he knew Latin pretty well for his time; he wrote in Latin. "Columbus is an eloquent man, a good Latin scholar," as the Portuguese chronicler Joao de Barros describes him. He knew also astronomy, geography and history, was versed in philosophy and was a kind of an expert in his knowledge of the Bible. He was well schooled in art, was a good designer and cartographer and was also a keen observer of the life around him. Furthermore Columbus had a very fine handwriting—another mark of a man who saw some good schools. "He could have earned himself a living with it if he wanted," says his son Fernando.

The question is now: Where a Genoese woolworker acquired such a knowledge, such a—for his time—splendid education? Bartolome de Las Casas, who possessed all personal papers of the Admiral and was redactor of his diary, said that Columbus came from noble parents and studied at the University of Pavia. This, of course, is excluded for Christoforo Colombo. This one was not noble nor is there any trace that he ever attended any school, much less the university. At the age of twenty-one Christoforo Colombo was described in 1472, as "woolmaker from Genoa".

Certain historians believe that he was a self-educated man who somehow "picked-up" his education and his knowledge while he was on the move. But this is hard to accept: The experts are of the opinion that the knowledge which Christopher Columbus exhibited could have been only acquired early in his life, not later when he was a grown-up man: Here we have the 15th century wool-weaver who became a low, simple seaman and for a time a pirate, busy in educating himself while practicing and pursuing those glorious and worthy professions! What is only left is that somebody should come up and declare that Columbus in reality acquired his knowledge thru a correspondence school! But if Columbus, indeed, "picked-up" somehow, somewhere, his education, what about his brother Bartolome? This one appears as a replica of his brother Christopher. He had the same fine handwriting, difficult to differentiate from his brother, he did everything Christopher did, he knew everything Christopher knew and even better according to many sources; he was an excellent Latinist—better than his brother. How and where did Bartolome "pick up" his fine education?

Then there is the third brother Diego, allegedly Giacomo Colombo. Notorial records in Genoa mention one Giacomo Colombo in 1484, when he was 16-years old, as an apprentice learning the craft of clothweaver. Three years later in 1487, the same Giacomo witnessed a deed and is described as a "clothweaver in Genoa". He was still in Genoa in the same profession in 1491.

But only two years later the third Columbus brother appeared in Spain and he was not Giacomo Colombo at all, but styled himself Don Diego Colon and he knew Spanish and some Latin too! Inclined toward religion, he eventually entered the orders and became a monk. It follows that he too had certain education.

* * * * *

But the greatest difficulty in the identification of Christopher Columbus the Admiral with Christoforo Colombo the Genoese woolweaver arises when it comes to the question of the language spoken by the official discoverer of America. The first item that strikes the eye of one researcher is the totally unexpected fact that Christopher Columbus when he arrived in Spain in 1485, spoke and wrote Spanish. He used Spanish and wrote in Spanish even long before he came to Spain and this was his personal, official tongue and the only language he ever used!

When he wrote to some Italians, including the Bank of Genoa, he wrote in Spanish; when he wrote to his right-hand man Father Gaspar Gorricio, allegedly an Italian but of equally obscure origins, he wrote in Spanish; he wrote in Spanish even to his own brother Bartolome!

Now, how did it happen that the Genoese woolweaver who received no formal education, never resided in Spain and never was in Spain, knew the Spanish language even before he came to Spain and knew it well enough to make it his official language?

Nobody has yet given a satisfactory explanation to this puzzle;

it is in fact impossible to resolve this mystery if we stick to the notion that the Admiral of the Ocean Sea, Cristobal Colon, (that is how, officially, he called himself) was the same Christoforo Colombo the Genoese woolweaver.

There are several really devastating proofs showing that Columbus was not the Genoese Christoforo Colombo but some other man who much earlier was living in Spain and in the service of Spain and who in 1485, came—in reality—for the second time to Spain:

1.) Columbus' own letter to the King and Queen of Spain in which he indicated that he was previously (much before 1485) in service of Spain. "I came to serve at age of twenty-eight," he wrote to the Sovereigns of Spain. This must have been much earlier since Christoforo Colombo the Genoese was 34-years old in 1485!    The tendency of pro-Genoese historians to overlook this declaration or to explain it by simply stating that Columbus forgot how old he was and made an error will not wash the question away. Such strait and precise declaration, potentially of crucial importance, cannot be disposed off so lightly by the generally accepted rules and methods of historical science. Are we really going to insist that five centuries later we know better how old he was when he came to Spanish service than he knew himself?

2.) That Columbus was previously in service of Spain or more precisely and likely Aragon, no doubt, before it merged with Castile into unified Kingdom of Spain in 1469, is also indicated by the fact that he was regularly described by the Court of Spain as an "extranjero" (foreigner), however, without specified nationality, yet with all this he was accorded both the title and the privilege of Viceroy and Governor General though the laws of Castile prohibited conferring such titles upon a foreigner, Nevertheless, he received those titles without ever being officially naturalized. He did not need it. Most probably he obtained citizenship in Aragon earlier (it is known he was involved in dynastic struggles in Naples which was ruled by the House of Aragon). That made him *de facto* a citizen of Spain after the merger of Castile and Aragon, though in the Kingdom of Castile he was still referred as "extranjero." It was custom in Castile to refer to all Aragoneses as "extranjeros." His brother Bartolome

no doubt had similar history and was accorded the title of Adelantado also without prescribed naturalization. That means they
were both once in Spanish Aragonese and then Castilian service.

This must be considered proven practically beyond doubt by
the fact that their younger brother Diego effectively needed naturalization to be eligible for any post in church hierarchy in
Spain and was consequently officially naturalized by the Sovereigns of Spain in 1504, so that he could receive, as the King
and Queen decreed, any ecclesiastic position and benefices
which may be conferred upon him. Why did Christopher and
Bartolome not need official naturalization to carry to legitimately
their exalted titles while Diego needed the naturalization even
for the most modest post in the Church of Spain?

The case of Bartolome is particularly instructive in this regard:
When Columbus was in Spain, after 1485, this one was in Portugal, England and France almost all the time until 1493, when
he finally came to Spain after his brother's return from his voyage
of discovery. Yet, like his brother before, when he came to Spain
Bartolome equally spoke and wrote Spanish and likewise this
was also his own personal, official and only language he ever
used.

Those are the facts, known facts, and on the basis of it is really
hard to avoid the conclusion that they both, Christopher and
Bartolome, were once before in Spain and in the service of Spain.
3.) That Columbus was not Christoforo Colombo, the Genoese
wool-weaver is confirmed furthermore by the fact that when he
came to Spain in 1485, beside speaking and writing in Spanish,
he also knew Latin and, interestingly enough, his Latin was a
Hispanized Latin which again means that he surely resided previously for considerable period of time in Spain during which
period he either learned Latin or accustomed himself to the use
of Hispanized Latin while in Spain.
4.) The profound Hispanization of Columbus before his arrival
in Spain in 1485, is proven by still another curious fact: When
Columbus settled in Portugal and married in Portugal he did
not give to his first-born son and heir (born in Portugal from a
Portuguese mother) the Italian-Genoese name of Giacomo nor
the correspondent Portuguese name of Diogo—he gave him the
Spanish name, Diego, which is hardly understandable if Colum-

bus was the Genoese wool-weaver Christoforo Colombo and was never before living in Spain.

5.) But certainly the most surprising thing about Christopher Columbus was the fact that he did not know the Italian language well. He understood it enough, he read it, but could not use it fluently in speech nor in writing. So far as we know Christopher Columbus never expressed himself in Italian. With Italians he always spoke in Spanish, even with his own brothers, supposedly Italian-Genoese like him. He communicated only in Spanish! There is documentary proof that Columbus did not know Italian well. He left it himself in a marginal note he wrote on the "Historia de Plinio" which was published in Italian in Venice in 1489. Reading the book he translated some sentence in Spanish in such manner that it shows clearly that Spanish, not Italian was his habitual language.[8] He thought in it, he counted in it, he wrote in it.[9] At the end of the book he decided, however, to put one note in Italian commenting about the discovery of the Island of Hispaniola. This note, less than sixty words in all, is precious for our knowledge of Columbus. His Italian language is poor and incorrect and what is most significant, there is a lack of Italian vocabulary; the Italian words just fail him and he inserts Spanish words instead; there is almost more Spanish in it than Italian![10]

The possibility that Columbus may have forgotten the Italian language is discarded because a grown-up man who leaves his country at the age of twenty-five cannot forget his mother tongue.

From this note, coupled with total lack of Italian in Columbus' personal and official papers, some historians drew a quite logical conclusion that Christopher Columbus could not have been an Italian because the Italian was not his maternal language.

The linguistic difficulty throws a large shadow over the notion of Columbus as Genoese. There is no way of disposing of it unless some monumental evidence is discovered. But the legions of "Columbus was a Genoese" partisans have, of course, put up an argument: Yes, they say, but we must consider that Columbus really never spoke Italian, he spoke only the Genoese dialect of Italian! So says even Ramon Menendez Pidal the noted Spanish scholar. The error of those historians (as, for example, the American Henry Harrisse) says Menendez Pidal was to assume that the maternal language of Christopher Columbus was Italian, while his language was a Genoese dialect![11]

Now, this is one argument which does not add any clarification to the "Columbus' case" while historically does a great disservice to the official discoverer of America. It is virtually a declaration that Columbus was in a sense an idiot! After all "Genoese" is still Italian language and one native Italian who speaks it certainly can use and understand some "regular" Italian. And Columbus did not live only in Genoa and did not know only the Genoese dialect. He knew a lot of Europe and all of Italy; He knew the Mediterranean as well as the Atlantic coast.[12] During his lifetime he met all kinds of Italians and was in all parts of Italy. He knew copiously and in detail the entire Mediterranean coast of Italy from Nizza to Naples and Sicily.[13] He also knew very well the Adriatic coast of Italy; he knew Venice and resided in Venice;[14] he knew Ancona;[15] he knew Lombardy and all the Northern Italy[16] where the "regular" Italian language predominated. Besides, he also read books in "regular" Italian (like that "Historia de Plinio").

Is it possible to assume with all this that Christopher Columbus, such a highly intelligent man who could learn foreign languages and even Latin, that he who was born and raised in Italy and traveled all over Italy was unable to use some "regular" Italian? Was he really that stupid to be incapable to grasp the general language of his own country and his own people? I believe this too must be considered too fantastic to be taken seriously.

Besides, even this proposal does not solve the problem: Columbus never used the "Genoese language" either. He never wrote in "Genoese" and there is not a single document which says that Columbus ever used "Genoese" in speech with anybody, not even with the members of his own family. Where is then that famous "Genoese language" of Columbus?

The Genoese try to explain this oddity by declaring that the Genoese dialect was not really used as language for writing and its use was generally avoided in conversation! This is the explanation in case anybody can understand this: First they explained that Columbus and his fellow Genoeses did not speak Italian, but the Genoese dialect which, in turn, they again say, they did not use!

So, what kind of language did those "mysterious" Genoese, particularly the common folks like the Colombos, use? One would suspect it was not Chinese! The linguistic question definitively remains unresolved. It is by no means certain that the Italian or the Genoese dialect of Italian was the maternal language of the official Discoverer of America.[17]

Even some otherwise pro-Genoese historians admit that the question of language is so serious it alone justifies several other hypotheses.

* * * * *

It is evident that the real ethnical background of Christopher Columbus remains clouded. Despite the well established notion of Columbus as Genoese—the notion created and maintained mostly for political reasons—it is still not certain nor proven that Cristobal Colon the Spanish admiral and Christoforo Colombo the Genoese wool-weaver were one and the same person.

And after all what was said about it before, there is also more: Numerous additional evidence against the conception of Columbus Genoese can be cited. To mention just some of it:

1.) The enigmatic person of Christopher Columbus becomes no less mysterious and unexplainable when his attitude toward Genoa and his relations with Genoa are examined. In the first place one can make sure that Columbus, himself, never declared that he was a Genoese. There are only two such documents in which Columbus allegedly said so. The first one, the alleged Military Testament of Columbus in which he declared Genoa to be his beloved fatherland is a proven and notorious forgery. The other one, his alleged Testament of 1498, is also a crude forgery based probably on Columbus' true testament which he made in 1502, and which has disappeared without a trace, surely, as Salvador de Madariaga points out, to be replaced by a fabricated one dated 1498, which was forged much later (in 1564), and in which all those items about Genoa and Columbus being born in Genoa were inserted.[18]

2.) While in Spain, Columbus was never officially described by the Court of Spain as "Genoese." This was contrary to then established custom by which after the name of a person, particularly a foreigner, his country of origin, province or place of birth was generally added. While other Genoese were regularly described as Genoese, Columbus was not; neither were his two brothers. He was usually referred only as "extranjero" (foreigner) without specified nationality. Now, the King and Queen of Spain were probably the only persons who knew exactly of which nationality was their secretive. Admiral. If they refused as a rule to mention him as a Genoese, while describing him as a foreigner, then it must be that he was not originally from Genoa.

3.) It is strange that Columbus never proposed his project of reaching India by going West to Genoa, his alleged native city which was a great maritime and mercantile power. Instead, he spent years of hardship in foreign countries trying like a beggar to sell his projects to Portuguese, Spaniards, English and French, but never to the Genoese. Finally, he gave the New World to Spain, the country which for some reason he liked the most and adopted as his homeland.

4.) Columbus never expressed any particular feeling and love for Genoa.[19] He never honored his alleged native country. There is no Genoese Island in America, no Genoese Peninsula, no Genoese landmark of any kind. Columbus made sure that everything in New World got Spanish names—it was only the glory of Spain (and of himself) he was interested in. Columbus' feeling shows that abundantly from all his writings.

5.) Columbus never expressed any interest in Genoa, never expressed any longing for Genoa and never thought of visiting Genoa. He stuck with Spain and died in Spain. His brothers too, remained in Spain and died in Spain. A year after Christopher's death, in 1507, his brother Bartolome made a pilgrimage to Rome. During his stay in Italy he never even thought of visiting Genoa! Some Genoese!

6.) Columbus' strange acrobatics with his own name also suggest that he was not an Italian-Genoese. In the space of seventeen years he had changed his family name five times. In Portugal, apparently, he called himself initially Columbo, then Colon; in Spain he changed it to Colomo, then to Colom and then finally adopted anew the form of Colon which was his official name. His brothers did the same and also called themselves "Colon." Now this is unusual for a Genoese and for Italians in general who were not accustomed to changing or refashioning their names. So why Columbus was doing it? Besides, the form of his name is perfectly good in Spanish too; there are many similar names in Spain and even the name Colombo appears somewhat later. So why did he call himself Cristobal Colon and ordered that all his descendants must call themselves "Colon?"

7.) Christopher Columbus never surrounded himself with Genoeses nor maintained any close relationship with them. This is quite strange for those who know the Genoese and Italians in general. He had no particular friend among them. The best and most loyal friends of Columbus were Diego Mendez, Gaspar Gorricio, Angelo Trivigiano and Miguel Ballester—none of them Genoese! Mendez, a Spaniard, was the closest and the most loyal of all his friends with the exception of Gorricio, the Cartusian monk from Seville, whom some believe to have been a native of Northern Italy and who in all probability was not originally an Italian at all. This one was more than a friend to Columbus, he was practically a senior member of Columbus' own family, while Trivigiano (also called Trevisan) was a Venetian and Ballester another Spaniard (Catalan).

Previously, it was pointed out with great fanfare, that Columbus did in fact have one close Genoese friend: Nicolo Oderigo, the ambassador of Genoa in Spain with whom he corresponded regularly. But this alleged correspondence (all written in Spanish!) which was always suspicious, has also been declared a forgery some time ago and no serious historian is using it anymore. Consequently, no Genoese was ever a close friend of Columbus.

8.) The conception of a Columbus Genoese is no less shaken by another of his own statements, the one that he was once a captain of a vessel in service of would-be King Rene of Anjou who was a pretender to the throne of both Naples and Aragon as was previously mentioned. In this case it does not really matter if this episode occurred around 1460, or sometime in 1472–1473. What matters is that this Rene was an avowed enemy of Genoa; therefore that statement of Columbus implies that he fought against his own country. This, of course, casts a certain shadow of doubt on Columbus as Genoese by birth. On the other hand if we take the second possibility: that this episode was invented by Columbus, i.e. that he lied as some historians also believe, still, we have to come to the same conclusion. For, if he was a Genoese, he would have, certainly, invented a different story. Undoubtedly, he would have said that he was in the service of somebody else, because if he was Genoese, he knew perfectly well that Rene of Anjou was an enemy of his fatherland and thus must have been aware that such a statement implying that he fought against his own country could have exposed him as a liar. Nevertheless, he made that declaration which means that he had no fear of contradiction surely for the reason that he did not consider himself to be Genoese.

9.) This was not the only time in his life that he fought against Genoa. It is known that he had no love for Genoa at all and that on one more occasion he fought against the Genoese. And it is known that Columbus sailed the seas with that French admiral and pirate Guillome de Casanove-Coullon who, incidently, was called Colombo in Italy and Colon in Spain and it is known that with him he attacked, in 1476, the Genoese mercantile fleet near the Cape of St. Vincent, thirty-six leagues from Cadiz.

For the partisans of the "Columbus was a Genoese" notion this obviously presents another difficulty. Evidently under the impression that it established a strong case against Genoa being the birthplace of Columbus, many pro-Genoese historians furiously maintain that Columbus was on board Genoese ships and fought for Genoa without presenting any evidence to support such a claim. All the evidence is however on the other side, i. e. that he fought against the Genoeses. Bartolome de Las Casas who knew much about Columbus explicitly says that Columbus sailed as a corsair with French admiral "in which company he sailed and remained with him for a long time".[20] Besides, the Italian scholars themselves who made an extensive research on the battle of Cape St. Vincent did not find among the Genoese crew anybody with the name Colombo. It is known also that Columbus' ship caught fire and that he jumped overboard and swam toward the shore with the aid of an oar which helped him to stay afloat and reach the safety of a shore. Furthermore it is known that in the aftermath of the battle the Genoese ships returned to Cadiz, the friendly Spanish port, but Christopher Columbus did not follow the Genoese and did not swim toward the friendly Spanish shore where, undoubtedly, a bad reception awaited him; instead, he swam toward the Portuguese shore from which the French pirate, the ally of the Portuguese, attacked. A few days later Columbus appeared not in Cadiz to join the Genoese but in Lisbon where the French corsair-admiral returned!

Hence, in 1476, at the battle near Cape of St. Vincent, Columbus fought against Genoa: He attacked and killed Genoese!

10.) The fact that Columbus was a pirate and that he operated with Portugal as his base makes it nearly impossible to take him for Christoforo Colombo, Genoese. This one, according to Genoese sources, came to Portugal in 1476, but Columbus, the future admiral, arrived in Portugal five years earlier, in 1471, and was based there since that time. This is indicated by the mentioned statement of Las Casas who said that Columbus navigated and kept company "for a long time" with this French pirate Casanove-Coullon-Colombo-Colon. This statement alone literally destroys the notion that Columbus was the Genoese woolweaver Christoforo Colombo. And curiously enough this is confirmed by Columbus himself: In one letter he explicitly declared to have been a resident of Portugal for fourteen years! (That means 1471–1485).

This is another statement which is giving the pro-Genoese historians many headaches for they cannot explain it, except to say that he probably "forgot" how long he was living in Portugal and made a mistake! On other occasion he "forgot" how old he was when he came to Spanish service—so they insist—here he also "forgot" how long he was in Portugal . . .

11.) There cannot be doubt that there is a certain mystery concerning the real lineage of Columbus. Bartolome de Las Casas, for example, is reluctant when it comes to the question of nationality of the Admiral. Although he gives him as Genoese he does not subscribe himself fully to this notion and therefore he simply quotes the Portuguese chronicler Joao (Juan) de Barros, himself an uncertain source, who only said that "as all affirm this Cristobal was of Genoese nationality".[21] Now, how is this possible? Bartolome de Las Casas possessed most of the Admiral's papers as well as his diary and personally knew his two brothers and one of his cousins, one certain Juan Antonio Colombo or Colon who was said to be from Genoa. (That is if that "Juan Antonio" was really his Genoese cousin!) Las Casas says that he had many conversation at large with this alleged cousin of Columbus, yet, Las Casas definitively does not know that Columbus was born in Genoa! (This much for those who staunchly maintain that Columbus was born in Genoa and even show the house in which he was supposedly born). The nagging question here, of course, is: Why Bartolome and Diego did not tell Las Casas where they were born and where their brother was born? Anyway, Las Casas obviously himself unsure and somewhat mystified reports only, always according to others (sic), that Columbus was born "somewhere" on the Genoese territory. What was the place and what name it had? Las Casas says: Nobody knows!

12.) The suspicion that Columbus the Discoverer was not Christoforo Colombo, Genoese is further nourished by the rather strange fact that he was able to hide from posterity his entire early life. Chronologically, Columbus is relatively close to our time; he was almost a modern man (died in 1506). We have an enormous knowledge of this historical period, practically everything from this time is known to us, yet, Columbus, one of the most famous and most discussed men in history, almost entirely escapes our knowledge. How is this possible? Now, if Columbus was what they say he was, Christoforo Colombo the Genoese wool-weaver turned sailor who navigated thru all the Mediterranean, the Atlantic and the Northern Sea, voyaged to Guinea in Africa, lived in Lisbon etc., he must have met in the course of such a busy and active career literally hundreds if not thousands of people who knew him from some place or other very closely, yet, when Columbus became the most celebrated man in Europe, nobody, and this must be emphasized, absolutely nobody, came forward, recognized this man and declared that he knew him, once met with him, associated with him, navigated with him and so on. He had no past, no acquaintances, no memories, no nothing.

This all suggests that Columbus was rather one complete

stranger, probably a foreigner of yet unknown origin, an adventurer who commuted from country to country, changed his allegiance, his name and his nationality as often as it was necessary and suited his purpose.

13.) Furthermore, even the Genoese documents are not above reproach. What those documents really show is that there were numerous families of commoners in Genoa called Colombo (nothing extraordinary, there were lots of Colombos all over Italy), and that in one of those the names of Christoforo, Bartolomeo and Giacomo are found. This even if true, does not necessarily mean that they were identical with those which in Spain called themselves Colon. It may be purely accidental: so numerous are the Colons and Coloms in Spain that the existance of those three names in one of such families also would not be anything extraordinary. It is possible that the usual identification of Columbus' brothers with Genoese Colombos stems exactly from one such combination and originated in Portugal where their Genoese namesakes, the simple wool-weavers and mariners also resided for a certain period. It just may be so, but this is, of course, purely a speculation. However, the truth is that those Genoese documents are certainly not conclusive. It must be said that most of this documentation is somewhat questionable simply because it is of later date not original. There are in fact some who doubt the authenticity of any of those documents and consequently doubt that any Domenico Colombo and any Christoforo, Bartolome and Giacomo in reality existed in those times in Genoa. On this one it is hard to agree but the noted Peruvian historian Luis Ulloa did create some uproar and some doubts in his book "Christophe Colomb, Catalan" published in Paris in 1927. He sharply criticized the reliability of Genoese documents in relation to Columbus and put a question mark on many of them. Ulloa noted that of all those 200 or so documents of supposed evidence only fourteen mention Christoforo Colombo or his brothers Bartolomeo and Giacomo of which seven for which it is said that the originals or certified copies exist, only in one which bears the date of September 10th 1489, the names of all three are mentioned together. In this document their father Domenico Colombo describes himself as a lawful administrator of his three sons Christoforo, Bartolomeo and

Giacomo which means he was looking over their inheritance, from which Ulloa deducts, if the document is authentic, that those three Colombos were minors clearly in care of their father and could not have been identical with Christopher Columbus and his brothers: Christopher was then a middle-aged man living in Spain (three years before the discovery), while Bartolome was in England.[22] This document is certainly confusing and obviously does not aid the Genoa case. And the fact that over the time a number of forgeries appeared with express purpose of showing that Columbus was a Genoese is of no help either. It only raises more doubts.

14.) Columbus never maintained any relations and any links with his alleged Genoese family though his alleged father, mother, his two brothers, sister, his uncle, his first cousins and numerous other relatives were all alive! Why Columbus otherwise so clanish, nepotic and fiercely loyal to his brothers and their families, never mentions, for example, his alleged father Domenico Colombo in Genoa? He was alive for several years after his alleged son discovered the New World, yet, died unrecognized, abandoned and alone! And if Columbus did not care for his father why did the Republic of Genoa not take care of him? If that poor Domenico was the real father of the Discoverer how did it happen that nobody in Genoa took note? His alleged son following his great discovery was the most celebrated and talked-of man in Europe. If that Domenico was his father he would have been, certainly, transformed into the most popular citizen of Genoa and the Republic of Genoa would have, surely, paid some public honor to him. But nothing of the kind: In 1494, nearly two years after Columbus' epochal discovery, that Domenico Colombo is an ordinary and common man in Genoa whom nobody recognized and as such Domenico Colombo, described as a wool-weaver witnessed the will of one of his neighbors and the other witness was a local shoemaker! If that Domenico Colombo was the father of Christopher Columbus is it possible that the Genoese notary would not have noticed that the witness is the father of the great discoverer and the Viceroy of the New World of the "Indies" and added something appropriate instead of marking him down simply as a mere wool-weaver?

15.) In regard to Columbus' alleged Genoese family it is necessary to point again to that Genoese document of September 10, 1489, in which Domenico Colombo declared himself the administrator of his three sons Christoforo, Bartolomeo and Giacomo. It must be noted that according to those Genoese documents the Colombos of Genoa were not exactly poor; they were solid middle class, even somewhat wealthy by the standards of those times. Domenico was a master wool-weaver and a member off the local guild; he was also a businessman and possessed a tavern in Savona. Through his wife the family also owned several buildings in Genoa. The important question here is: Who inherited all this? Christopher Columbus and his brothers, certainly, never went to Genoa and never inherited anything in Genoa! And there is another equally important question concerning those alleged members of Columbus' family in Genoa and numerous relatives: Where have they all disappeared?

Or is there a possibility that maybe, just maybe, they never existed after all? Or, which is more credible, that they may have existed but were not his family and in no way related to him?

These are the legitimate possibilities to be considered for the evidence is quite impressive . . . Even that falsified Columbus' testament dated as of February 22, 1498, made for the express purpose to "prove" that Columbus was indeed Genoese, inadvertently, points out that Columbus in reality had no family in Genoa at all. Here is the relevant passage from this alleged transcript from the alleged Testament of 1498, which was made (forged) 58 years after Columbus' death: "Item: And I order the said Don Diego, my son, or the person who will inherit the said entail-estate to keep and support always in the City of Genoa one person of our lineage, who will have there a home and a wife . . . "

Now, this is interesting. First, of course, it shows that the testament is a forgery because this provision in his alleged will was never carried out simply because such provision was not present in Columbus' true testament which he made in 1502, and which has mysteriously disappeared. He ordered no such thing. Second, why Columbus ordered that one person "of our lineage" should be maintained in Genoa, when there were already, according to the same Genoese documents, numerous persons of his lineage there? Why Columbus does not mention also other members of his alleged family, like his other brother, his sister, his uncle and first cousins who were also supposed to be there? And why he does not mention here his alleged Father, Domenico, who was also alive at that time in Genoa?

Why Columbus cares so much and does everything possible for the members of his family which are with him in Spain and does absolutely nothing for those which are in Genoa? He never even mentioned them in his lifetime! Some Genoese!

Obviously, even the forgers, long after Columbus' death, were unaware that Columbus was supposed to have numerous family in Genoa. In any case, even if all those Colombos in Genoese documents really existed, no relation between them and Christopher Columbus has been established.

16.) And finally, another knock against the Genoese conception of Columbus is represented by the surprising fact that Columbus' own sons did not know who their father was nor from where he came!

This oddity nobody can explain because his sons were not little children when Columbus died. When he died his older son and heir Diego was 26 years old, while Fernando, his later biographer was eighteen. The certainly mysterious nature of Columbus' case thus cannot be denied. If Columbus was a Genoese and if he was a proud and patriotic Genoese as some, incredibly, insist, despite the evidence to the contrary, why he did not tell it to his own sons?

Fernando Colon, his younger son and biographer, says in his writings that the question of the origin of his father intrigued him, but the Admiral resolutely refused to divulge his true origin and his nationality to his own sons and "because I was very young I was hesitant to question him out of filial respect" says Fernando. He speculated that his father may have been a relative of that French admiral-pirate Guillome de Casanove-Coullon, called Colombo in Italy and Colon in Spain, obviously because of the similarity of name and the fact that Columbus navigated for several years with this French corsair. In other places Fernando speculated that his father descended from an ancient and illustrious Roman family named Colon which later changed its name to Colombo (sic) and he said that the noble family of

Colon-Colombo had their tombs in Piacenza! The historians have found nothing to substantiate those speculations of the son of the Discoverer. Fernando Colon, of course, knew about the widespread belief that his father was Genoese-born. To verify those claims he actually traveled to Genoa and personally searched in the City of Genoa and its surroundings for the origin of his illustrious father and found no trace at all of his father's family![23]

To summarize it all: We really still do not know, for certain, where Columbus was born. His origin and ethnic background remain open to questions and, understandably, to various hypothesis.[24]

# PART II.

## Resolving the Enigma: Columbus' Role in the Discovery of America

Of course, the logical and cardinal question is inevitably, posed by itself: Why did Christopher Columbus hide his origin and his past? Why was he reticent about his past life and about his family and his country?

Nobody has ever proposed a cogent explanation for this unusual and extraordinary conduct of Columbus which is absolutely crucial for finding the truth about Columbus, the man and his discovery. The truth, no doubt, traces back to the year 1471, when Christopher Columbus, then an unknown foreign adventurer, soldier of fortune and opportunist, after many years in Italy and Spain eventually found his way to Portugal sometime during 1471, (he explicitly declared to have been a resident of Portugal for fourteen years), where he associated with that French admiral-corsair Guillome de Casanove-Coullon and financially with some Italians from the large Genoese colony in Lisbon and probably here and there passed for a Genoese wherever it suited his purpose. In 1478 or 1479, he married Doña Felipa de Perestrello e Moniz and went to live with her to her mother's home on the Island of Porto Santo near Madeira, maybe, as some scholars believe, with the intention to found a line of hereditary captains of the Island of Porto Santo. It was here that Columbus came into possession of knowledge of the existence of lands or islands across the ocean, more precisely of the existence of Hispaniola and some other islands which were discovered by chance in 1484, by the Spanish pilot Alonso Sanchez de Huelva, who was driven West by a storm while on his way from Canaries to Madeira. The Spanish pilot after taking the altitude and making other observations turned for home and barely succeeded in reaching Madeira with only four survivors. On Madeira they were taken to the home of Christopher Columbus who was there something of a local celebrity (being a foreigner and big talker). Columbus offered his hospitality to the five surviving sailors, but they all died within few days. However the Pilot before dying informed Columbus of his discovery and left him instructions and a navigational chart as they say in gratitude for his hospitality.

Armed with the knowledge of the lands across the Ocean, Columbus presented himself at the Court of Lisbon in 1484, and asked for a fleet to go to discover those islands which he estimated, because the earth is round, to be a part of India. But having carefully omitted his source of information, passed to him by Andalusian pilot, he hastily constructed some arguments in favor of such voyage to make it look as a product of his own intelligence. But the arguments of this foreign adventurer who probably was not a professional mariner, were poor as it could have been expected. He was in fact ridiculed at the Court of Lisbon. Turned down there, he passed to Spain where he spent seven years trying to interest Spanish sovereigns in his projects. Finally, in desperation, without doubt having disclosed the secret of new lands to the King and Queen of Spain, he obtained the fleet and sailed Westward in 1492.

This is simply and shortly the story of Christopher Columbus and his so-called discovery of America. Originally, Columbus was only searching for those Atlantic islands which Alonso Sanchez de Huelva charted him on Madeira. The rest of the story is only a later invention of Columbus himself, and of his son Fernando and his adulator Bartolomé de Las Casas. This is how the "discovery" of Columbus was made. This is how the discovery is viewed also by some other historians. Of course, such thinking is revolting to the legions of those who believe that Columbus must have been the original discoverer. Naturally, after being hailed for so long as the legitimate discoverer, adulated and glorified often beyond recognition by numerous historians and writers of any kind it is hard for someone today not to be impressed by such long list of authors, which maintained thru a such long period that Columbus was a genuine first. The idea which was cultivated and believed for centuries, as it is in case of Columbus, dies hard, as we know from experience. Any attempt to prove the contrary logically draws rage and indignation. And there are also some additional reasons too: first, nobody likes to be proved wrong in his beliefs, secondly, due to the importance of the discovery of America and impact which it had on Western civilization and on history as a whole, many people just cannot get it in their heads that in one such monumental historical happening, as was the discovery of the New World, some kind of deception was involved. How can a man who opened a new era in human history be an imposter? The third reason and the main reason, consciously and subconsciously, is political. Politics has prevented so far a more realistic and more critical and objective look on the origin of the discovery. Nationalistic rivalries, chauvinism and political considerations often influenced our understanding of the problem.

There can be hardly a doubt that America was discovered in 1484, by the Spanish pilot Alonso Sanchez de Huelva who passed this information to Columbus. The name of the real discoverer of the New World is not certain, it was given more than hundred years later by Garcilasso de la Vega, though it seems quite credible. But, that an anonymous Spanish pilot reached the New World several years before Columbus with his small caravel—"Atlante" is said to have been the name, with crew of seventeen was a fact well known in Columbus' time. Besides, the Indians from Cuba informed the first Spanish explorers that a ship with bearded white men was there not many years before Columbus fleet of Santa Maria, Niña and Pinta appeared.

American author Samuel E. Morison maintains that a ship cannot be "blown across" the Atlantic, if it happened he says, she can only drift across if all her sails have been torn apart, and without the sails she would be unable to make a return.[1] But the story is however not improbable as another author Clements R. Markham noted.[2] In fact, what Morison says seems to have just happened to the caravel, that she drifted across after losing most of her sails or all of her sails. There she was repaired or patched up. The fact that it took the caravel so much time to return, several months of hardships during which most of the crew died and barely succeeded in reaching Madeira gives full veracity to the story. The caravel was indeed damaged and made a risky and desperate run for home with little sails, probably makeshift ones at that.

Bartolomé de Las Casas, the greatest defender and adulator of Columbus, whom some authors accuse of alternating or deliberately falsifying the diary of Columbus and other papers to make him good and credible, himself mentions this story which circulated in Hispaniola in 1500, and admits that the story may be true. He noted the fact that the Indians from Cuba had the memory of a ship with white men arriving there some years before:

"It is said that one caravel left Spain carrying merchandise to Flanders or England . . . which ran into a terrible storm and by force of it was thrown across and found herself near those (Caribbean) islands and that this ship was the first to have discovered those islands. There are some arguments to support this version: the first is that among those who came here first it was a common custom, as I said, to talk about it and treat it as certain fact which I believe came from someone who knew it, from the mouth of the Admiral himself, or in all or in part from some words he heard from him. Secondly, . . . we who came first to the island of Cuba . . . it was this one where the neighboring Indians of this islands had recent memory of having seen the other white bearded men, like we are, arriving to this Island of Hispaniola not many years before us. And this the Indians from Cuba could have known because it is only 17 leagues the distance between the two islands and Indians communicate every day with their barks and canoes . . . Having discovered those islands in this way, if this was so, they turned for Spain . . . most of them died from exhaustion, hunger and illnesses, only the remaining few reached Madeira, where all subsequently died. The pilot of the said ship either for friendship he had before with Christopher Columbus, or because he was solicitous and curious about this business and tried to inquire from which place they came and for what reason, because he suspected there is some secret which those who came wanted to keep for themselves . . . or maybe for pity seeing him in such bad shape and so needy, Columbus offered him shelter and hospitality in his house where after ten days he died, but which in recognition of the old friendship or for that good and caritative work, seeing that he is going to die, divulged to Christopher Columbus everything what happened and gave him instructions and a navigational chart which they brought with them, where the altitude and the position of the island which was found were all put dawn in writings.

This was what was said and opined among us . . . and held for certainty as a reason which effectively and without doubt moved Christopher Columbus".[3] Francisco Lopez de Gomara in his work "Historia General de las Indias" (1553) ridiculed the story circulated by Columbus and his adulators that he came to a conclusion that the lands across the ocean exist from his own studies by reading classical literature. For Gomara this was too fantastic (which it certainly was), Columbus therefore, said Gomara, only followed the discovery of the anonymous pilot who discovered the Hesperides Islands and revealed it to Columbus on Madeira.

In his "Historia Natural y Moral de las Indias" (1592), José de Acosta noted: "And so it happened in the discovery in our time, when this mariner (whose name we still do not know, for an enterprise so great is not credited to other author but a God), having found the New World by virtue of terrible storm, left the news of this great discovery to Christopher Columbus as a payment for his good hospitality . . . "[4]

The Inca Garcilasso de la Vega gives the more precise account in his famous "Royal Commentaries" about the Incas of Peru (published in Lisbon 1609). He gives the details and names the pilot who furnished the news and the map of his discovery to Christopher Columbus on Madeira. He identified him as Alonso Sanchez de Huelva. Though he wrote it more than hundred years after the official discovery, Garcilasso's account is so straight, precise and authoritative that it must have been derived from some excellent and reliable source. The Padre Juan de Mariana gives a similar account in his great work "Historia General de España" (1609).

English historian Lord Francis Verulam, Viscount of St. Alban in his "History of the reign of the King Henry the Seventh" (published in London 1622), noted that Columbus received the news about the lands across the Ocean from a Spanish pilot who died in his house, which Columbus subsequently suppressed to make it all look like his own discovery . . .

Gaspar Estaco in his book "Varias Antigüedades de Portugal" (Lisbon 1625) says, that Columbus did nothing else, but traveled to those lands as everybody is doing in actuality, that is to say, he simply traveled to a place which he knew to be there, while another Portuguese, Simon de Vasconcellos, in his chronicle about the work of the Jesuits in Brazil noted the death of Alonso Sanchez in the house of Christopher Columbus to whom he gave "his own navigational chart where the land was marked".[5]

The veracity of the story of Alonso Sanchez de Huelva, his discovery and his meeting with Columbus in which he revealed the existence of the lands on the West is confirmed also by a tradition which is preserved to this day among the inhabitants of Portuguese island of Madeira. In Funchal, where Alonso Sanchez, the real discoverer of America died, the people of the town still show today the house of Juan Esmeraldo as a place where the meeting between him and Columbus occurred.[6]

That Columbus did not discover the New World but only followed Sanchez's discovery is confirmed by number of convincing proofs:

1.) Columbus' own attitude, his frantic efforts and those of his adulators to prove that he, many years before the discovery, came to a conclusion that there is a land in the West by studying classical and other literature. If we are to believe this results that Columbus already as an apprentice woolweaver and teenager discovered the Western route to India . . . His son Fernando even pretended that his father, through study, conceived the notion that between Europe and Asia lies an unknown continent which he then went to discover! . . .

2.) Total lack of information on Columbus' past and on his experience as a seaman: Numerous authors of international fame take for a fact Columbus' own declarations about being a mariner for many decades and we are told by those writers that Columbus navigated everywhere, Mediterranean, Atlantic to Bristol and Flanders, Northern Sea to Iceland with the Portuguese expedition of d'Azambuja to Guinea and below the Equator in Africa and so on, and that it was in the 1470's that he (remember an uneducated Genoese woolweaver in his early twenties!) became convinced of the existence of the lands across the Atlantic and that he already had conceived his grand design of reaching India by sailing West!

Now, to present things like that and treat them as proven facts is to make one veritable mockery of historical science. We know nothing, absolutely nothing, about Columbus as a mariner, except what he said himself. He is the only witness—and what an unreliable witness he is—everything he said carries no weight, all that he said is, as is well known, cloudy, contradictory and fantastic and cannot be confirmed by one contemporary source. According to the basic accepted laws of historical science nothing can be taken as a truth, unless it can be confirmed by an independent and authentic source, everything else is just guessing and speculation. And this must be emphasized: absolutely not a single certain and authentic proof exists which shows that Christopher Columbus ever, before 1492, navigated as a crewman on any ship! Nobody ever navigated with him, nobody ever knew him as a fellow mariner, there is absolutely no record of Columbus as a seaman, unless he navigated all those years as an invisible ghost . . . It is obvious, and this must be accepted as a fact, for not a single document against it exists, that he was not in reality a mariner by profession, only an occasional seaman and pirate for some time. Coming into possession of knowledge of the islands of the New World, given to him by the Pilot of Huelva, he invented his mariner's past to be able to claim the discovery, as an enterprise of his own intelligence and mariner's skill. This is the only explanation, for if he was already in 1474, as some say, sure about the Western route to India and allegedly discussed it with Toscanelli, why he waited a decade until 1484, when America was discovered by somebody else, to present his project?

Obviously, he learned most of his navigational knowledge after 1484, by studying and consulting with experienced mariners. In fact a number of experts who have studied Columbus as a navigator are quite skeptical about his seamanship, some of them indeed believe that Christopher Columbus was not a professional mariner at all.

3.) His alleged correspondence with Paolo Toscanelli in which no serious historian believes anymore and which Columbus wrote to himself after Toscanelli was safely dead (in 1482): The first "Toscanelli letter" was addressed to Cristobal (Spanish name!) Columbo, which infers that Columbus was then in Spain or Portugal and was dated few days after the June 24th, 1474! That letter is Columbus own forgery (he left this letter in his own handwriting as an alleged copy of Toscanelli's letter to him). Of course, Christoforo Colombo the Genoese woolweaver, them 23-years old, was not yet then in Portugal, neither he called himself yet "Cristobal". The questionable letter from Toscanelli was sent to Fernan Martins, Canon at Lisbon on June 24th, 1474. This letter Columbus saw much later and copied it and pretended that Toscanelli at this time sent him also a copy of it. In the second alleged letter Columbus was again addressed as "Cristoval".

The "Toscanelli correspondence", invented by Columbus himself, could not have been made for any other purpose than to strengthen Columbus' false claim that he was the first who discovered the New World, because he allegedly had this idea almost twenty years before and discussed it with the prestigious man of science, Paolo Toscanelli!

That Columbus needed a recourse to forgery testifies clearly that his idea of discovery originated only in 1484, when somebody else discovered it and left him in knowledge of it.

4.) His residence on Porto Santo and Madeira: Many authors see this stay of Columbus in Madeira as some kind of a step toward his discovery of America, because, here, according to them, he had better opportunity to prepare himself for his projected exploration. In other words he deliberately choose Madeira as a springboard for his great enterprise. Madeira—they say—was a logical step in his way to discovery. This ridiculous notion was propagated also in his time by his adulators. This is what Las Casas says:

"As the days passed Columbus' mother-in-law understood that he had an inclination for navigation and cosmography . . . and she told him that her husband Perestrello also had an inclination for navigation and was sent by Prince Henry of Portugal to populate the Island of Porto Santo which was shortly before discovered . . . and that the said Bartolomé

Perestrello from here hoped to discover other islands . . . and had instruments, notes and charts which his mother-in-law gave to the said Christopher Columbus, who was very happy to see all this, and to study it. With this it is believed his natural inclination for study of cosmography and astrology was induced and revived and also made him inquire into the practice and experience of navigation which the Portugueses were undertaking to Mina de Oro and the Coast of Guinea.[7] Later historians took it from him as a logical, natural and sacred truth. Yet, Salvador de Madariaga, who himself strangely believes that Columbus already in 1470's visualized and prepared his Westward voyage, has completely destroyed Las Casas' story. Bartholomeu Perestrello, the late father-in-law of Columbus was not a mariner at all and did not receive the captaincy of the Island of Porto Santo (which was hereditary), for his sea-prowess and merits, but for favoritism, because his two sisters were the mistresses of the most powerful man in Portugal, Dom Pedro de Noronha, the Archbishop of Lisbon who was of royal blood.[8]

Hence, there were not such things as notes, instruments and charts left by Perestrello which allegedly made Columbus so happy. He was not there to prepare any exploration. He came to Porto Santo-Madeira to his mother-in-law's home as a freeloader (for 6 years!) hoping also to inherit her captaincy. Thus his arrival in Madeira could not have been for the reason that he saw in it an ideal base for the exploration of Western sea. Before 1484, Columbus was never interested in exploration of anything; his only interest was concentrated in acquiring money and position for himself. Las Casas unintentionally divulged the truth in his already mentioned note about the instruments and charts of Perestrello: "With this it is believed his natural inclination for the study of cosmography and astrology was INDUCED and REVIVED and make him to INQUIRE into the practice and experience which the Portugueses were undergoing . . . " In other words in the previous period of his life, preceding his arrival in Madeira, Columbus was not interested, nor engaged in any maritime exploration when his "natural inclination" for the sea had to be "induced" and "revived" on Porto Santo! This "inducement and revival" provided in 1484, the unfortunate Spanish pilot Alonso Sanchez de Huelva who left him in possession of the knowledge of his own discovery.

5.) Columbus own statement that he had lived for fourteen years in Portugal and that, for fourteen years, he kept talking to the King of Portugal about his project of reaching India by going West (but the King turned his ears elsewhere): This is the statement which is giving many headaches to Columbus specialists, particularly to those who maintain that Columbus was both genuine Genoese and genuine discoverer. The general tendency is to avoid it, to ignore it, for they cannot find one reasonable explanation for it. But, we cannot dispose of a fact in such an un-historical way by sweeping it under the rug, as it is popularly said, and forget about it. The statement is there and we must deal with it, be it true or untrue.

Now, if the statement is true we can in this case eventually accept the proposition that Columbus, many years before, conceived the idea of going West and that he may have been the original discoverer. But in this case his identity with Genoese Christoforo Colombo would be destroyed. That one was not in Portugal in 1471, but in Genoa, as we know from the same Genoese documents, was working as a wool weaver and was only 20-years old.

On the other hand, if we accept that the statement is untrue i. e. that Columbus lied, we can then eventually agree that he could have been the Genoese Christoforo Colombo, but then in turn the idea that Columbus was the original discoverer of America would be just about destroyed.

6. Columbus knew of the existance of Hispaniola and some other islands in the Caribbean and communicated this secret to the King and Queen of Spain: We know that Columbus tried in Spain, just as he had in Portugal, with various arguments constructed by himself to obtain a fleet for his voyage to the West, but was equally unsuccessful and was finally turned down after more than five years of insistence. We know that, when he was finally refused by the Court, he disclosed, in desperation, no doubt, the secret informations he had about new lands to his friend Fray Juan Perez of the Monastery of La Rabida to whom he secretly "opened his heart". That Friar wrote then, to the Queen and Columbus was immediately recalled. The existance

of the lands he proposed to "discover" was never questioned
after that and he was furnished his desired fleet. Thus the Fray
Juan Perez, the King and the Queen were the ones who obviously knew the real secret of the discovery. Of course, they
never disclosed it for the information was given to them under
the oath of secrecy. That Columbus disclosed the information
he received from the Pilot of Huelva is beyond doubt, for how
could the Court of Spain, so many years incredulous and reluctant, now suddenly overnight change its mind and accept Columbus' propositions with no questions whatsoever asked
anymore?

If Columbus did not know precisely that there was a land in
the West how could he have been, him, a poor foreigner, without
a penny, so adamant and uncompromising in his demands?
How could have he posed to the Sovereigns of Spain, the proud-
est monarchs in Europe such arrogant, humiliating and unheard
of in history demands and conditions? What he asked for himself
was plainly unbelievable: He asked to be named Admiral of the
Ocean Sea (Atlantic to the West) and that it be hereditary in his
family; he asked that his rank and privileges be the same as that
of the Admiral of Castile, a person of royal rank and blood. He
asked that he be named Viceroy and Governor General of all
lands he will discover and of all those which will be discovered
in future and this all was also to be his, hereditary and in perpetuity, that is to say he asked for a half of the globe for him
and his family plus financially one-tenth of all income from all
lands which will be discovered!

Incredible as those arrogant conditions were, it is even more
incredible that those conditions were accepted by Spanish
Crown, which proves that he had secretly divulged to the Court
the previous discovery of the Pilot from Huelva and proved
beyond any doubt that there is a land which had been already
and effectively discovered.

Those who insist on Columbus as the genuine discoverer are
obviously uncomfortable in the face of those facts, but they have,
of course, come out with an "explanation". Well, they usually
say, the Court changed its mind and accepted all the propositions and demands of Columbus because he probably showed
them the map of Toscanelli. Certainly, they say, he showed

them that letter which Toscanelli wrote in 1474, to Fernan Martins, Canon at Lisbon and said that there are islands and lands to be discovered by going West, a copy of which letter Columbus either also received from Toscanelli in 1474, or later saw in Portugal and copied (or stole)!

Now, this is another explanation which, I believe, most of people will agree must be the most ridiculous explanation ever given in history: Are we going to believe that the Court of Spain changed its mind overnight, accepted all those fantastic demands of Columbus and granted him in perpetuity the rights on a half of the Earth just because this foreign adventurer and beggar pulled out of his pocket one questionable letter—some old rubbish—of some Toscanelli, one for several years already dead astronomer from Florence, in which this Toscanelli (of whom those on the Court of Spain probably never heard) opined that there is a land to be discovered in the West![9]

The only thing left to make comedy out of history is to declare that when the Genoese woolweaver brandished the old letter of the Florentine astronomer (not the original but only an alleged copy of it made by Columbus himself!) the entire Court of Spain sang Te Deum with King and Queen on their knees thanking God Almighty for the revelation of the letter of Toscanelli! Why should this eighteen-years old letter of Toscanelli carry such decisive weight and why should it carry any weight at all? If Columbus indeed presented this letter as his main argument the only effect he could have made on those of the Court of Spain was to make them laugh for what Toscanelli allegedly said in this old letter was basically nothing new, just plain old rubbish. In those times of discovery when the fever about discovering the unknown and distant lands was sweeping thru Europe, similar opinions and maps like that, made by many experts and self-styled experts, circulated by the hundreds in Spain, Portugal, Italy and some other Western countries, each one showing various lands to be discovered in the West, such as, for example, Antilia, Hesperides Islands, Brazil, St. Brendan Isle, Cipango (Japan) and so on, as is well known. Everyone who was then engaged or interested in navigation and exploration had some maps of this kind. (Martin Alonso Pinzon who accompanied Columbus, as a second in command, and whose merits for the voyage of 1492, are equal to that of Columbus, if no greater, also had one similar map which he brought from Rome and showed to Columbus before they took of for the New World).[10]

7.) Columbus' previous positive knowledge of the existence of the lands in the Caribbean is proven beyond doubt and this proof is to be found in those famous Capitulations of Santa Fé (Columbus' contract with the Crown of Spain) where, among others, the famous sentence appears which says that the satisfaction or recognition requested by Columbus for "this what he has discovered" (de lo que ha descubierto) in seas of Ocean and for his present (1492) voyage which he will make in their service is granted by the King and Queen. This is the original document which states clearly that Columbus had previously discovered some parts of the New World, and is now (1492), merely going again there to make further discoveries, which means he had positive knowledge of the lands in the West. Against this proof the "Columbus was a genuine discoverer" partisans cannot really offer any argument except to scoff at it or ignore it as if this is the natural, scientific method and way of resolving and disposing of one historical problem. Some others tried to build up the theory that Columbus probably "pre-discovered" America sometime before. For example, the Peruvian historian Luis Ulloa proposed the hypothesis that Columbus discovered America fifteen years before in 1477! According to Ulloa Columbus was then in the service of the King of Denmark and called himself then—John Scolvus! This, of course, belongs to the realm of fantasy. America was discovered by the Andalusian captain Alonso Sanchez in 1484, who passed this information to Christopher Columbus on Madeira and this was the source of Columbus' knowledge of the existence of lands of the New World and this is what he communicated in the end, in secret, to the King and Queen of Spain, which made them change their mind and accept his propositions and conditions, however they found them insulting and arrogant. It is possible he told them that he was himself personally present in the voyage of Alonso Sanchez to the Caribbean or that he was an associate of his. In any case, by presenting himself as the only survivor or associate of the first discovery he could have claimed that discovery rightfully as his own and thus he is mentioned in those Capitulations as the one who has already discovered some lands in those parts which he is now going to visit again . . .[11]

This original document, alone, represents unquestionable proof that Columbus knew where he was going.

8.) Fray Bartolome de Las Casas, the admirer, defender and glorifier of Columbus, cannot completely avoid the impression that Columbus had previous knowledge of the lands he was going to "discover". Unintentionally, perhaps, he let some rays of truth escape to the light. For example, Las Casas said that Columbus had such certainty that he was going to find that what he found as if this all has been situated and locked in one single room of which he (Columbus) had a key . . . "

Las Casas also said this: "But, as I understood, that when he decided to look for one Christian prince who would help him and support him, he already had such certainty that he will discover the lands inhabited by people, as if he had been already personally in those lands (of which I certainly do not doubt) . . . "[12]

9.) Columbus possessed navigational instructions, directions and a chart showing Antilia (Hispaniola) and some other islands which the Pilot of Huelva gave him on Madeira. It is known that Columbus had papers and charts which he jealously guarded for himself. This could not have been in any way the dubious map of Toscanelli (which probably never existed), for he had no more reason to keep it secret after he, allegedly, showed it to the Court of Spain. Hence, the belief that Columbus navigated according to the supposed map of Toscanelli is plain nonsense. He navigated following the instructions given to him by Alonso Sanchez on Madeira and he took exactly the same route by which that Spanish pilot arrived at Hispaniola in 1484. This is why Columbus when he went to his voyage of "discovery", instead of going West as it was expected, surprisingly and unexpectedly sailed South to Africa and anchored at the Canary Islands, a move which still baffles the experts of navigation. Various explanations are given for this curious move of Columbus, but it just happened that the Canary Islands were the starting point in 1484, of the Pilot of Huelva in his unintentional voyage to Caribbean. Columbus took the same direction navigating West in the latitude of the Canary Islands. And there really ends all the mystery of Columbus' supposed discovery.

10.) That Columbus received information about the new lands across the ocean from that Spanish sailor who died in his home on Madeira is indicated further by the fact that Columbus did not come to Spain in 1485 voluntarily: He fled from Portugal. The Portuguese authorities were after him! The question is, of course, why? He was never accused of committing some criminal act. The matter, no doubt, was that the news of the arrival of surviving members of the crew of Atlante—the Alonso Sanchez' caravel—at Madeira, their ending and their connection with Columbus leaked around and the Court in Lisbon belatedly realized that this foreigner had come into possession of certain important secret and wanted to seize him and his secret. That's why the Portuguese King John II, was later so eager to entice Columbus to return to Portugal by promising him many things, as seen from the royal letter delivered to Columbus in Seville in 1488.

In any case the news about the arrival of Atlante leaked out from Madeira. Even before Columbus went to his voyage of alleged discovery, seemingly, there was certainty of the existence of the lands across the ocean, precisely, of the existence of Hispaniola (Antilia). In 1965, the ABC of Madrid published a map reportedly from 1485, (published also in the New York Daily News) which shows Antilia (Hispaniola) in a place where it is supposed to be!

Finally, the previously mentioned testimonies of the Indians from Cuba of having seen a ship with bearded white men not many years before Columbus, a fact which even some Columbus glorifiers cannot deny, shows definitively that America was originally discovered some time in 1484. Christopher Columbus only followed, eight years later, this discovery according to the instructions and a chart he received in Madeira from the unfortunate Spanish pilot from Huelva.

* * * * *

This then would answer the questions about why Columbus hid his real origin and his entire early life.

For his reticence to talk about his origin and his secrecy about his early life, three popular explanations have been given by various believers in the "Columbus was a genuine discoverer" notion. They proposed, as it is known, three possible reasons why Columbus allowed that a veil of secrecy cover his origin and his early life:

1. Columbus came from a poor family and he wanted to hide his humble origin.

2. Columbus was a pirate for some time and wanted to keep his piratical past secret.

3. Columbus was a Converso and wanted to hide his Jewish origin because he thought it might harm his grandiose projects.

All those three "explanations" only raise the already large number of nonsenses which were said about Columbus for the following simple reasons:

1. It is unbelievable and plainly unacceptable that Columbus, just because his family was poor (the Colombos from Genoa were, in fact, middle class) and came from the ordinary strata of society, would hide his origin and his early life to the point of renouncing his own country, his own family and his own identity. Beside, Columbus had no possessions of any kind anywhere and often referred to himself as a "poor man" and "poor foreigner". Columbus was not ashamed of poverty.

2. As for his once being a pirate, this, of course, was no reason for him to keep secrecy. Piracy then was often (depending on situation and conditions) almost an honorable "profession". Even many high-born aristocrats often engaged in piracy to become subsequently honored men, courtiers and statesmen of their respected countries. England, for example, began to build its overseas empire strictly thru piracy, as it is well known (and from which even Queen Elizabeth I had her own cut of the loot). Besides, Columbus did not hide his piratical past and his association with that French corsair Guillome de Casanove-Coullon who was also one of those kind: Privately a pirate, officially an admiral of his sovereign the King of France!

All this was no secret and no shame. This is why both his glorifiers, Bartolomé de Las Casas and his own son and biographer Fernando Colón mention the period in which he was engaged in piracy practically as a mark of distinction.

3.) The third reason which some advance is that Columbus was

of Converso origin and feared that this might create some obstacles to his projects in Spain. Well, one cannot see why this
bothered him. Even if he was of Converso origin (which would
be very remote in any case—some hundred years back), why
should this have hurt his chances in Spain?

Now, such thinking does not take in consideration what Spain
really was in the time of Columbus. The country was dominated
by Conversos. The converted Jews held all kind of posts in the
Spanish Realm from the lowest ones to the highest ones and
many of them were "instant converts" who converted in 1492,
(outwardly only), to escape deportation. The Conversos dominated the Court of Spain and held number of key positions and
this was the pattern which had been in existence effect for centuries. In fact, for generations Spain was literally governed by
Conversos.[13] Some of those powerful Conversos in the Court,
like for example, Luis de Santangel and Gabriel Sanchez, helped
Columbus. And not only the political structure of the Spanish
state, but even the structure of Catholic church in Spain, the
most rigorous in Europe, was completely dominated by Conversos who set the tone and held all the key positions. Juan de
Torquemada, Cardinal of St. Sixt was Converso for example,
and the Inquisitor-General Cardinal Tomas de Torquemada,
himself, was of Jewish origin too, according to numerous
sources. Almost the entire Church of Aragon was entrusted into
the hands of Conversos.[14] The chief chaplain of the Queen was
Alonso de Burgos, a Jew, and Queen's personal confessor and
favorite, Hernando de Talavera, who exercised an immense influence over her. was of Jewish origin.[15] In fact almost the entire
royal household of Queen Isabella was Jewish. The converted
Jews were in charge of all matters of the Court of Spain, financial,
military and ecclesiastic.[16] In short there were no obstacles in
Spain to anyone of Jewish origin who converted to Catholicism
even if this conversion happened only 24 hours before. (In his
voyages to America Columbus had numerous royal commissioners with him who were recent converts). According to contemporary thinking and principles in Spain the Catholic faith
made all inhabitants of the Spanish Realm equal regardless of
their race or national origin.

So why was Columbus so reticent about his past and his own family? Can we imagine that he renounced his native country, his own family and his own identity just because his family happened to be of a (very remote—century ago) Converso origin which meant absolutely nothing in Spain in his time? This is impossible! Anyway, if Christopher Columbus was Christoforo Colombo, Genoese, he had nothing to worry at this point: He was Catholic and born Catholic, his father was Catholic and born Catholic, his grandfather was Catholic and born Catholic, so what then?

Clearly, only one possibility is left: Columbus hid his identity, his origin and past life in order to protect what was most important for him—his life's achievement, his glory, his New World, his hereditary viceroyalty, governorship and admiralship. We may assume that if he had disclosed his true origin and his past, lacking any serious record of a professional mariner who was never previously connected with any exploration he could have been exposed as a liar and impostor and one who had nothing to do with the discovery. His numerous enemies who envied him would have been, certainly, happy to dig into his past if he gave them an opportunity! After all, the rumors and speculations that he was, in fact, preceded in his discovery by someone else was not a later invention, it circulated in his own time. That is, he was viewed with suspicion from the very beginning. Thus this unknown foreign adventurer who obviously spent, previously, some time in Italy and may have been partly Italianized and as such found himself in Lisbon's large Italian-Genoese colony where he had some financial dealings with some Genoese individuals and through them probably also with the Bank of Genoa, was naturally taken in Portugal for an Italian-Genoese and he was maybe tacitly passing here and there for such because it suited his purpose admirably. But, most probably, he was not from Genoa and he, himself, personally, never insisted in being from Genoa and never said, in fact, that he was a Genoese. Neither the Court of Spain, undoubtedly aware of his true origin, ever mentioned or identified this international adventurer as a Genoese . . .

Most probably he came originally from a country adjacent to

Italy, more precisely from the Croatian region of Dalmatia which was for centuries owned by Venice and from which a number of famous "quasi-Italians" or Croato-Italians originated, including among them the most famous of all, Marco Polo, Columbus' own idol.[17]

# PART III.

## Political Aspects of the Discovery of America Throughout History and Today

*WHY WAS COLUMBUS GIVEN CREDIT FOR THE DISCOVERY?*

The question left to be discussed is, of course, why the discovery was attributed and given to Columbus and not to the Pilot of Huelva despite the conclusive proof showing that he preceded Columbus in his discovery? And also the question is why the role of Spain in this enterprise is usually played down, often almost ignored?

The reasons for all this originate from political considerations and from imperialistic rivalries, past and present. Since Spain had the good luck to be presented with the New World, that country has become the object of widespread international attacks, physical and propagandistic, in a tacit conspiracy which the other envious rival powers mounted against her. This all gave rise to a so-called "Black Legend" about Spain and her conquest and rule in America which is still propagated today, even though Spain has not had a presence in America since the last century. But, the "Black Legend" remains generally in force because it is still politically needed, it must be kept alive to justify also that which we call today Americanism, that is it is necessary to justify those past movements for independence and subsequent seizure of power by the renegade Spanish colonial oligarchy under the auspices of their foreign mentors and benefactors which thru the invention of the idea of Americanism in fact succeeded in their original purpose: The expulsion of Spain from the New World and her replacement by somebody else. Thus the reasons for vicious characterization of Spain and Spanish action in the hemisphere, deliberate distortions of history and wild exaggerations, in treating Spanish-American history. So, the "Black Legend" about Spain in America is still in force and the Columbus question, such as it is presented; is an integral part of this nefarious legend from which it cannot be separated nor understood unless we examine objectively and without passions the entire Spanish action and rule in America because the "Black Legend" and political undertones which go with it is also the basis for the "Columbus Legend."

Of course, the conquest of America by Spain and her rule in America is too lengthy a subject to be presented here. It should only be said that with the emergence of Americanism in the 18th and 19th centuries it became, more than ever, a political necessity to paint the Spanish action in the hemisphere in the worst possible colors and to denigrate and diminish the role of Spain in the discovery as much as possible and even it was attempted to disassociate completely the people of Spanish America from Spain.

With such historical anti-Spanish bias and anti-Spanish propaganda it is not surprising that the Hispanic population of the New World was never called by its proper name, Spanish-American or Hispano-American, until very recently. The obvious aim of such efforts was to destroy the only possible basis for the union of Spanish America, the basis which rested on common ties with Spain thru blood, language, history, culture and religion for eventual united Spanish America would have been probably too big to be subjugated or dominated successfully. Thus the general offensive against everything Spanish went on despite the fact that Spain was liquidated as an American power and reduced back in Europe to the status of a second or a third class country.

Of course, all that criticism and anti-Spanish propaganda which is still in current use is not aimed today, in reality, against the country of Spain. That propaganda is aimed now primarily, thru the use of Spain, at the Spanish-speaking nations of the hemisphere which succeeded Spain. All former Spanish colonial rivals participated in it and are still in it today.

France, who had designs of her own in Spanish America and was not disposed to be left aside, also tried to extend her own influence through repeated military intervention of which the infamous occupation of Mexico is the best remembered. It was, in fact, France who, for her own use, coined the phrase, "Latin American" instead of Spanish-American. This description was quickly accepted by others too and this invented, unhistorical and distortive name is widely used today. Effectively, this description reduced the Spanish-American population to some sort of undeveloped and semi-civilized bastards with no fathers, no past, no history and no culture (because everything that was Spanish now was no more theirs), thus they became just a mass of human beings of uncertain parentage who could only be vaguely described as Latin (whatever that means).

France, of course, lost out to her more powerful Anglo-Saxon rivals, United States and Great Britain. The United States, however, did not succeed in destroying Spanish language and culture in America (as they did later successfully in the Philippines), but succeeded in establishing their almost total political and economic domination with the tacit agreement and cooperation of England by which agreement the English recognized the United States as the guardian of common Anglo-American interests in Americas as a part of global Anglo-Saxon policies.[1] Thus, near the end of the 19th century the American Secretary of State, Richard Olney, was in position to declare that the United States are practically sovereign in this hemisphere. The English, of course, were themselves generously allocated a big slice of American cake too. The Monroe Doctrine was never invoked against them, in fact, the Doctrine worked for their benefit.[2] What's more, the British fleet was in reality the ultimate guarantor of the Monroe Doctrine. They kept their enormous territory of Canada and other possessions and, furthermore, they were allowed to make some additional conquests in Hispanic America. In the domain of economic expansion the British also had free hands. And not only were the British to stay, but France and Holland were also allowed generously to keep their existing American possessions, some of which they still own today. Significantly, those finally expelled from the Hispanic-American continent were the only two Hispanic countries, Spain and Portugal, which, by historical, ethnical, cultural and many other reasons were the only ones who had at least some rights to be there . . .

But, this was really the eventual purpose of Americanism and then can there be any wonder that the question of Columbus and of the discovery of America was also treated with the same traditional anti-Spanish bias and hostility? Not really, considering the noted tendency exhibited by historians throughout the times (with few exceptions) to treat historical questions in a manner which usually coincides with traditional views and interests of their respective governments. Hence, the question of who really discovered America five centuries ago, surprisingly as it may look, is in fact treated with political sensitivities and thus with the same unavoidable prejudice against Spain and the Spanish-speaking Americans in general.

The United States government not only made Columbus officially an Italian, but went even much further by officially making the entire discovery of America an exclusive enterprise of Italians and Italy! The day of the discovery in 1492, is officially celebrated in the United States as the day of Italians and Italy with members of American government, including usually the President himself, honoring it regularly. This is really something unparalleled in history no matter who Columbus may have been, Italian or not, because the discovery of 1492, was only and exclusively an enterprise of Spain and the Spanish people to whom in all fairness all credit is due: The man who led the voyage of 1492, to the New World, regardless of where he was born, was a Spanish admiral who called himself by a Spanish name, Cristobal Colon, whose sovereigns were the kings of Spain, who was in command of a Spanish fleet and hoisted the Spanish flag on the newly discovered land, and who took possession of the New World for Spain. Nobody can deny this, otherwise, analogically speaking, it can be then proclaimed, with full justification, for example, that the greatest voyage of modern times—American Moon landing—was exclusively a German enterprise belonging to the German people and the German state, because the head of the American space program was the German-born Wernher von Braun (the former V-2 expert) who was furthermore aided by a team of no less than 58 other German-born scientists who designed practically everything including the Saturn V rocket which took the Americans to the Moon. Of course, the American people would take such an interpretation as an insult, but the United States, which a long time ago proclaimed themselves the champion of Americanism and present themselves as "big brother" are doing exactly that to their "younger" American brothers who happen to be of Spanish language and ancestry (some brother!)

The reasons for this official stand of the United States government, of course, stem not from its knowledge of history but from political considerations: There was always a certain feeling in the United States that the Spanish-Americans have to be kept low lest they become unmanageable.

The English-speaking people settled permanently in America very late (1620), long after the Spaniards (1492), and even the others, the Portuguese and French preceded them. They have been thus somewhat sensitive to this potential "Johny come lately" syndrome. The total triumph of Americanism throughout the hemisphere which made the English-speaking United States the originator of Americanism and the dominant power of the New World did not change this perception at all. The ruling, always predominantly, Anglo-Saxon establishment of the Northern colossus, despite its might, deep inside, always feared that the "Latin" variety of Americans may someday reject Americanism and go back to their Hispanic roots. And that fear is justifiable. Today, in fact, in the United States, the most powerful English-speaking country in the world, English is actually losing ground: Spanish is rapidly becoming the second official language of the nation and the Hispanics, throughout the hemisphere are slowly beginning to take another, more critical look at their post-1810 history, that is, at the "American era" and are making a much more favorable appraisal of their pre-1810 Hispanic past and roots. In short, Hispanism is on the ascendancy again albeit a slow one. The geopolitical impact and implications of this trend on the United States and even the world could be enormous in the future!

Today, the Hispanics or "Latins" constitute the absolute majority of population in this hemisphere generally speaking. And in the United States they are already the second acknowledged minority (after the Blacks). They may be even the first counting the Puerto Ricans from the island (which are U.S. citizens) and the illegals. And in the not too distant future, the number of Hispanics, according to some estimates, may, due to various factors, reach as much as 70 million—more than a quarter of the population—while their number in the rest of the hemisphere is expected to jump to some 600 million! Furthermore, if this trend continues, by the year 2,025 there will be over a billion Hispanics. So what then?

The far reaching implications of those likely figures are of the first magnitude for the future of everyone and the United States in particular. Even more so when combined with the fact that those people have been here since Columbus, that is, since the official discovery. (Naturally, the Indian part, now largely Hispanized, was always here).

The uneasiness of the "Anglos" from the North is thus understandable. This is why Columbus had to be an Italian and even more, this is why the discovery had to be more or less credited exclusively to Italians and Italy, not because the Italians were loved, but only to avoid the dreadful prospect of having to see it all credited to Spain and thus also to the people of Spanish extraction in the Americas. And this is also why those who suggested that after all Columbus may have only followed the previous discovery of a Spanish pilot from Andalusia have been given the proverbial silent treatment. Included in such treatment were also some of America's own historians who have expressed similar convictions. This explain also the reasons why Columbus was treated so generously by most of other historians and writers and made into a hero of Americanism while other Spanish conquerors and explorers have been vilified and damned. It is enough, for example, to mention how Columbus was compared with two other most famous Spanish conquerors and explorers, Hernan Cortez and Francisco Pizarro. For comparison, Hernan Cortez, the brilliant conqueror of Mexico, had never the slightest idea or intention of enslaving the Indians. He was not an Indian killer and torturer as he was often maliciously portrayed by numerous distortions of historical facts.[3] Cortez was not cruel to Indians and, in fact, was loved and respected by most of them.[4] How else could he have rallied around him almost all of Mexico and even many Aztecs against the Aztecs after he was expelled from Tenochtitlan with three quarters of his small Spanish army slaughtered and he found himself a defeated soldier and survivor of a massacre seeking refuge among the friendly Indians of Tlascala? He rebuilt the war-ravaged country as it never was before and extended the borders of Mexico as never before way into today's United States. His infamous American and republican successors (and detractors) after 1821 squandered, lost or sold much of this territory to foreigners! A product of his time, Cortez saw the future of Mexico religiously, culturally and politically linked and integrated with Spain and Western Europe—he did not want a Mexico of conquered and conquerors, of slaves and slave-owners. In consequence he wanted the country to be ethnically and racially integrated exactly as Mexico has become. Far from hating the Indians and free from any racial bias he effectively promoted and encouraged mixing and intermarriages between Spaniards and Indians: His principal lieutenants, all of them Spanish noblemen, married Indian girls, so did most of his soldiers and he, himself, had a recognized son with an Indian girl (Malinche) . . . The same can be said for Francisco Pizarro, the fantastic conqueror of Peru. As it is known, his great conquest produced less bloodletting then did for example one local campaign against the Indians two centuries later in today's United States when the Indians in West Virginia were subjugated.[5] Pizarro's testament, found and published in Paris in 1936, shows an entirely different Pizarro than the one often described by malicious pens: He cared sincerely for prosperity and peace in Peru and exhibited concern for the well-being of all, especially for the Indians, Blacks and poorer, less lucky conquistadors.[6] He had three children by an Indian girl (sister of Atahullpa) and took care that they received a good education. The eldest one he made his heir. He made all his three half-Indian children legitimate in 1537, by the decree of Spanish Crown.[7] And it must be noted that Pizarro was only an old, battle-scared and crude simple soldier who was once a swineherd and who did not even know how to write!

On the other hand we know that Christopher Columbus, a shadowy figure, an impostor and confirmed liar was the first conquistador in America. He was the first who made war on

Indians, the first one to kill the Indians and the first one to exploit brutally the Indians. It was under his rule and responsibility that the population of the Caribbean Islands began to dwindle. It was Christopher Columbus the very first one and the only one who proposed that the Indians be made slaves. The idea was all his and it was he who rounded up the Indians and shipped them to Spain to be sold as slaves causing the good Queen Isabella to burst into a rage when the first shipment of 500 slaves arrived. The infuriated Queen sent them back to America and wrote angrily to Columbus asking: "Who gave permission to my Admiral to make my subjects slaves"? Even this did not deter Columbus. He kept scheming, for the rest of his life, how to circumvent it—so much was he obsessed with the idea of making the Indians slaves and selling them for money that in his subsequent two remaining voyages to the New World he had to be, repeatedly, warned in advance by the King and the Queen to not bring back any slaves with him!

Yet, with all this, those two brilliant conquerors, Cortez and Pizarro, just because they were Spaniards, have been depicted in many historical books often in hair-raising manner, while Columbus, just because he was generally believed to not have been a Spaniard was, in most of the cases, raised to the stars, glorified beyond recognition, praised and described as a great credit to the human race, as a perfect picture of Christian knight and there were even some luminaries, like Roselly de Lorgue and Leon Bloy, for example, who went as far as to propose this very first conquistador and enslaver of Indians for sainthood! This, yes, is indeed hair-raising. Needless to say that if things were different, if Christopher Columbus was a confirmed Spaniard, while the pilot who preceded him was a Genoese or any other non-Spanish nationality, that all the credit, a long time ago, would have been given to that Pilot in 1484, while Columbus would have been described by those same historians as one of the worst conquistadors, murderers and impostors in history. This description of Columbus admittedly may be a little bit too harsh, due, mainly, to the efforts of the writer not to appear—for obvious reason—too partial to Colubus in any way, because throughout history, the case of Christopher Columbus was played excessively either for political reasons or for the matters of national pride. Some say Columbus did this under the pressure of his creditors. It may have been so. But, even if true, this does not absolve him from the guilt.

This is also why Martin Alonso Pinzon, the real hero of the 1492 voyage, is usually overlooked or diminished in stature by most of those historians. A professional mariner he, himself, contemplated such a voyage and went to Rome and to Papal Curia to discuss about it. Pinzon was looking to reach, by going West, Cipango (Japan). And he even had the means to do it all on his own. He owned the two caravels, the Pinta and the Niña. But when Columbus went around with royal ordinance looking for help and for a crew Pinzon gallantly put himself and his two ships at his disposition. He also rounded up the crew of the expedition. Pinzon went as Columbus' second in command and was the master of Pinta, while his younger brother Vicente Yanez commanded the Niña. It did not take long for Martin Alonso to become disenchanted with Columbus when it became obvious that this boastful and hungry foreign adventurer was out to appropriate the himself absolutely everything. Columbus even grabbed the prize set by the King and the Queen for the one who saw the land first—10,000 maravedis—a pittance, which he stole from one poor sailor, Rodrigo de Triana from Seville (he gave it later to his mistress). Columbus claimed that the night before he saw some lights flickering at a distance; therefore, he said he was the one who really saw the land first! The poor mariner protested to the Court of Spain, but Columbus won this one too with the Kings. Disappointed and deeply hurt by such a glaring injustice in a Christian country Rodrigo de Triana left Spain and settled among the Moslems in North Africa!

When Columbus—poor pilot as he was—lost the Santa Maria by running her over a reef, he took over the Ninā. (Now, probably in an effort to save something of Columbus' reputation as a seaman, someone is saying that Columbus was drunk on board at the time and that a 14-year old was at the helm! Be it even so, it certainly shows what kind of a pilot and admiral Columbus was!). On their return he and Martin Alonso became separated by a storm and then it became a race of who will be the first to reach Spain with the big news. Martin Alonso landed first at the coast of Galicia from where he sent a dispatch to the sovereigns informing them about the discovery. But they answered him that they preferred to hear about it all from Columbus and directed him to proceed back to Palos. Martin Alonso Pinzon entered Palos with the Pinta six hours after Columbus. Nobody waited for him! Exhausted from the hardships of the voyage, rebuked by his sovereigns and dejected, the luckless Martin Alonso went to his nearby country home, fell ill and died shortly afterward from a broken heart! He realized, belatedly, that the glory of this discovery which could have been and should have been his was grabbed entirely by this fast talking foreign adventurer of whom nobody knew much. Worse, he realized that it was he, himself, who contributed the most to that adventurer's triumph! Martin Alonso Pinzon was the dupe of the discovery! Enough for a man to die from a broken heart!

Some historians have tried to make out of Martin Alonso some sort of a villain. You see—they say—he wanted to take away the glory which rightfully belonged to a great man—the "great man" being for them Columbus, of course. But if there was a villain in the discovery it was certainly Columbus himself. A confirmed liar, he was an impostor not only as a discoverer but most probably also as a mariner: The only time we know for sure that Christopher Columbus ever commanded a ship was when he stepped on the deck of Santa Maria in 1492. On the other hand Martin Alonso Pinzon was a man of integrity and for a difference from the obscure Columbus a man with a clean record and an open past. He was a professional mariner, an expert navigator who participated and distinguished himself in naval wars with Portugal and explored in Africa: he sailed along the Coast of Guinea. Without him Columbus would have never made his "discovery". Martin Alonso made the voyage of 1492 possible. It was he who gave and outfitted the two caravels, Pinta and Niña, and it was he who gathered and signed the crew for nobody wanted to go with Columbus. As one witness testified later during the litigations: "If Martin Alonso had not given two ships to the Admiral, he could not have gone through with his expedition, for no one knew him and he would not have found men to go with him"[8] Thus Martin Alonso Pinzon was the real hero of the discovery of 1492, together with his brother Vicente Yanez. His stature and merits have been diminished deliberately in most of the countries traditionally opposed to Spain for the express purpose of making Columbus look great and beyond reproached as much as possible. For the same reasons his younger brother, Vicente Yanez Pinzon, has been also virtually passed over by those Columbus enthusiasts. On his merits he ranks as one of the greatest navigators in history, maybe even the best of them all: A co-discoverer of America with Columbus in 1492, he later, in expeditions of his own discovered Brazil in 1499, and was the first European to see the world's mightiest river—the Amazon. In 1506, he discovered and explored parts of Central America and in 1509, he pushed down along the coast of South America as far as Argentina. He discovered more land than Columbus, who never ventured farther than the Caribbean Basin. Yet, he is hardly known in non-Hispanic countries. The public, in general, has never heard about him!

This is also why the year of 1984, has passed without notice, the year which in reality marked the 500th anniversary of the discovery of the New World by its real discoverer Alonso Sanchez de Huelva while many are already busy preparing for the celebration in 1992, which will mark, with great fanfare, the 500th anniversary of the discovery that was not. Really, if there was ever an injustice in history, it was here, probably the greatest hoax and fraud of all times. The anatomy of this historical injustice is well known today. It all began in or about 1484, on the Portuguese Island of Madeira where an obscure and unknown foreign adventurer who called himself with many names, one for every different occasion, counted leisurely his days in the home of his widowed mother-in-law, Dona Isabel Moniz, and at the expense of his mother-in-law. This man was Cristobal Colon, alias Colombo, Columbo, Colomo, Colom and whom the English-speaking world calls Columbus. It is here that Columbus learned about the land across the ocean, more precisely about Hispaniola, from that mysterious but very real Spanish pilot. It was here where Columbus made his "discovery". The eventual voyage of 1492, was only a repetition of Alonso Sanchez' unintended trip to the Caribbean. Some years later, another obscure adventurer, the Florentine, Amerigo Vespucci, who was not even a seaman by profession at all, "explored" some parts of the New World. He was another of those foreign quacks the hospitable Spanish nation received and employed in those times. It is not really known what part he explored, if any, but it is known he loved to brag about the countries he never saw, exploits he never accomplished. He was probably the champion braggart and liar of his time. And a few years later, an unknown, second-rate German cartographer named Martin Waldseemueller proposed that the New World be named America in honor of the braggart!

Though the Spaniards, the discoverers and the sole legitimate owners of the New World (save for Indians, of course) never called the new continent, America, the name caught on simply because others wanted it to be known under such name. The reason for it was very important: Spain owned the New World, a very unpleasant fact for some other European powers which had colonial ambitions of their own and were stunned by the good luck the kings of Spain had. They wanted part of the action too. Thus the New World whose discovery was the most important event in history and changed the destiny of humanity did not receive its name in the honor of its real discoverer (Alonso Sanchez), nor even of its official discoverer (Columbus), nor in the honor of the country which made the discovery (Spain), but was named in the honor of another obscure impostor who had nothing to do with it at all!

This historical injustice was perpetrated strictly in deference to political considerations. Thus the question of who was Columbus, or even much more important, who really discovered America, remains very much a political issue today too, and it can be eventually resolved only when political equations in this hemisphere change. That is, when the growing Hispanic population in the New World, which once was exclusively the Spanish World, achieves enough cohesion and strength to be in position at which the United States will have to pay attention to it more than to everything else on this planet. That day, due to various hemispheric and global factors and especially the geopolitical and strategic considerations is in fact rapidly approaching: It now seems inevitable that the United States is destined to become, officially, a bilingual, English-Spanish speaking country, like it or not,and that some hemispheric union, some sort of a dual Hispanic-American transcontinental empire is in the future. And in such a future the old historical cliches about not only the origin of the discovery but also about the exploration, conquest and the rule of Spain in the New World will have to be examined more objectively and realistically and eventually replaced. And that applies in particular to the question of Christopher Columbus and his alleged discovery of America. Only then the political aspect of this discovery can be shed and the entire case viewed purely as an academic question left for the historians to debate. And it will be only then when, no doubt, what today looks fairly evident but politically embarrassing would be recognized; namely, that America was really discovered in 1484, by the Spanish pilot Alonso Sanchez de Huelva and that Christopher Columbus eight years later simply repeated that feat by navigating according to instructions he received from that unfortunate Spanish pilot on Madeira.

# PART IV.

## The Real Ethnic Background of Christopher Columbus; A New Hypothesis

The speculations about the origin of Christopher Columbus, the official discoverer of America, have been many in our century. Rarely was there a man in history who caused so much excitement and so much controversy and, rarely, was there a man in history who was so known and yet, in the same time so much unknown. The fact is that the historians are today, five centuries later, still at work to put together the scanty pieces of evidence which were left about Columbus. Of course, the general belief is that Christopher Columbus was an Italian, Genoese. There is numerous evidence to support such belief, yet, it is by no means proven, beyond doubts, that the Discoverer was indeed a Genoese. Much of the evidence contained in Genoese papers is questionable, most of the documents are neither originals nor certified copies; in fact, those few documents which are the most favorable to the "Genoa case", implying that Columbus came from Genoa, are either proven forgeries or suspected of being forgeries and are disputed by many scholars. Furthermore, as was mentioned before, many things we know for certain about Columbus, including several statements of his own, contradict the Genoese evidence. Among many things, in particular, is his surprising knowledge of Spanish before his arrival in Spain, his equally surprising poor knowledge of Italian, which he never used, and, again, his no less surprising good knowledge of Latin is absolutely unexplainable by the existing data in Genoa which say plainly that Christoforo Colombo at age of 22, was still working as a woolweaver in Genoa. And that's only a small part of what's unexplainable.

Besides, even the Italians, at least in what concerns the real birthplace of Columbus are not unanimous. Apart from Genoa, many towns on the Ligurian Coast and in other provinces of Italy also claim to be the birthplace of Colombus.

The difficulties with which the Genoese conception of Columbus is confronted, of course, strengthen the arguments of the scholars from the opposite side, the Hispanites, those who insist that Columbus was in reality born somewhere in Spain. Numerous such theories have been put forward with various degrees of credibility. Perhaps the best known one was that of the Peruvian historian Luis Ulloa who made Columbus a Catalan rebel named Joan Bautista Colom, the one who then became, according to Ulloa, Johannes Scolvus, a mariner in service of the King of Danmark, for whom he explored the Northern Sea and discovered America in 1477. He then transformed himself into Cristobal Colon and came back to Spain to ask the Sovereigns of Spain for a fleet to discover the unknown lands across the Ocean which he had already previously discovered! The amazing thesis of Ulloa may look fantastic, but his book, "Christopher Colomb, Catalan", published in Paris, in 1927, did have some success. While Ulloa did not prove that Columbus was a Spaniard-Catalan, he, however, somehow shook the authenticity as well as the reliability of many Genoese documents. After Ulloa's work some scholars began to look at Genoese documents with somewhat more reservations.

However, there really does not exist any substantial evidence showing that Christopher Columbus was a Spaniard: He was always referred to officially as a foreigner in Spain, he always called himself a foreigner and although his Spanish became, with time, excellent, Castilian was not his native language. Thus, the evidence for "Spanish Columbus" is weak and insufficient and equally contradicts many of Columbus' own declarations, although it is not entirely excluded.

Actually, in our time, a somewhat popular thesis is the so-called Converso or Jewish theory. This theory mainly arose from the discrepancies of existing data, both Spanish and Genoese. It was proposed that the contradictory data originated from the fact that Columbus' family descended from Spanish Jews who were converted to Catholicism some three or four generations before, and that both Genoese and Spanish data can be reconciled if we accept the proposition that Columbus was a Converso. The most notable of such theories was put forward in 1940 by the great Spanish scholar, Salvador de Madariaga, who did the most to popularize the thesis that the Discoverer of America was of Jewish extraction. This "Converso theory" would make Christopher Columbus Genoese-born whose great-grandparents came from Spain (Catalonia), but were Spanish Jews. This ingenious theory, thus, accords Columbus three origins in fact, Italian, Spanish and Jewish; i. e. it gives something to everybody to make everyone happy. But the Converso theory cannot solve the problem. There are no documents to support this hypothesis and the existing indications for Columbus' Jewish origin are also very weak and insufficient. This theory, in fact, does not add practically anything new to the old questions. It still confines the case to two basic alternatives: Either Genoa or Spain. (There are also some other historians who believe that Columbus may have been of Jewish extraction but maintain that he was born in Spain).

And this is not all. Many others claimed Columbus too. The Portuguese, for example, consider Christopher Columbus routinely to have been in reality a Portuguese navigator. However, they do not credit him with the discovery. According to them, America was discovered twenty years earlier, in 1472, by another Portuguese—Joao Vaz. This is what they teach officially in their schools. In the Columbus controversy the French were not absent either. And how can an international dispute, of any kind, pass without them! The French historians have noted the fact that Columbus sailed for several years as a corsair with that French admiral-pirate, Guillome de Casanove-Coullon, who was known as Colombo in Italy and Colon in Spain. They have also noted that Columbus' son Fernando speculated that his father may have been a cousin of that Admiral-pirate. For some Frenchmen this is enough—et voilà—Columbus was a Frenchman! Lately, in the "Who may Columbus have been" guessing game a new entrant from a wholly unexpected part of Europe registered—the Poles from the rather cold North, who suddenly became sailors in the sunny Mediterranean and in the tropical seas of Atlantic. Some Polish researchers read Luis Ulloa's work "Christoph Colomb, Catalan" and became fascinated by it. They accepted the first proposition of Ulloa that Columbus was Johannes Scolvus who was in 1477 in the service of the King of Denmark, but rejected his second that he was originally the Spanish rebel Joan Bautista Colom. The Poles derive the name Scolvus as coming from the then Polish town of Kovno. (Kaunas) According to Polish theory, Columbus was Johannes Scolvus and he was in turn Jan of Kovno. America, thus, was discovered by a Polish sailor named Jan of Kovno, who is mistakenly called today Columbus, Colombo or Colon!

And there were still many more: Columbus was said to have been also a Greek, an Irishman, an Armenian, an Englishman, an Arab and even a Turk!

Of course, none of those theories proved anything. The case is still basically confined to the old proposition: Either Genoa or Spain, with most of the people believing it was Genoa.

To determine the real national origin of Columbus, I believe, a radical departure from the established beliefs must be made. We should assume that Christopher Columbus was neither Genoese nor Spanish-born and look somewhere else for the origin of mysterious mariner. From the data we possess it is clear that the country of Columbus' birthplace could only have been one which was close to Italy and very much influenced by Italy and which, at the same time, had strong ties with Spain. There is only one country in Europe which fits that description: Croatia, the neighbor of Italy. The Adriatic littoral of Croatia, particularly Dalmatia, was thru centuries tightly linked with Italy. In fact, there was little difference between Dalmatian Croats and Italians—the intermixture between Italians and Croats was often such that throughout the centuries it was frequently difficult, even impossible, to differentiate between them.

Thus a Croatian hypothesis or, maybe, better described as a Croato-Italian hypothesis, comes into being.

Of course, Columbus was said to have been a dozen things in the ethnic sense.

Yet, while many of the claims about this or that origin of Columbus were rather of sensationalistic nature with little or no evidence to support them, and which are naturally pointed out to credit this or that nationality for the discovery of America, this book is not of this kind and has no pretensions at all to claim anything for the Croats. In fact, as it was seen previously, it is rather critical of Columbus and his achievement; it does not even credit him with the discovery. More precisely, this book points out that the discrepancies of data and mystery which surrounds Columbus stem primarily from his rather obscure and questionable role in the discovery and not from his obscure social or ethnic background.

It is really hard from those few uncertain documents which were left on Columbus to figure out many things. Nevertheless, thru careful examination, thru detailed detective work, it is possible to find out a wealth of indications showing that the man whom we call Christopher Columbus and who called himself Cristobal Colon was in reality an ingenious and so far unknown Croatian adventurer who came thru Italy.

It may be very useful to make one detailed historical investigation back in Europe in various Croatian towns and archives in Dalmatia which I was unable to do from this place (New York) at this time. However, the evidence for a Croato-Italian origin of Columbus and for his true role in the discovery which I have put forward here in this book, I believe, is good enough for a Croato-Italian hypothesis to be taken seriously, for certain indications are, unexpectedly, so strong, so surprising that, in my modest opinion, I cannot see how this evidence can be ignored.

To understand better the real possibility that Christopher Columbus may have been Croatian-born and that such a hypothesis is entirely warranted, indeed, inevitable, we must further examine, shortly, the relations and intermixing between the Adriatic Croats and the Italians. The Croats settled between the 4th and 7th centuries the former Illyrian provinces of Roman Empire. Thru this they came in contact with the local Roman-Italian or Romanized, mainly Illyrian population, which in the following centuries they absorbed completely. The Croats received their baptism from Rome, circa 642, and the first apostle among them was an Italian, John of Ravenna (Giovanni di Ravenna). This one became the first Archbishop of Split and thus the first Metropolitan of Croatia. The Croats settled even in some regions which were never for certain an integral part of the ancient Kingdom of Croatia. The Croats colonized Istra (Istria) yet we know that only a small Eastern part of this peninsula (to the river of Raša) belonged to the Kingdom of the Croats in 753, and after. The main Western part of the peninsula changed hands but ended up being most of the time up to 1797, a Venetian territory. But its population was mainly Croatian and the testimony for that is that the original Croatian Glagolitic alphabet which was used here in the earliest times and it is precisely here in Istra that some of the oldest examples of Glagolitic scripture have been found (8th century). It is known from Venetian sources, for example, that the road from Pazin to Poreč in Western Istra was called in 1030, "Croatian Road"; in 1145, according again to Venetian sources, the Mayor of Pula (Pola) was a certain Peter the Croat. In the 15th century, Eneas Silvio Piccolomini, who was previously there as a Bishop of Trieste, before becoming the Pope Pius II, said this about Istra: "The Istrians are today Croats, though in maritime cities they use the Italian language."

(Istra is today too ethnically overwhelmingly Croatian and is territorially a part of the present "Socialistic Republic of Croatia".) Now, after the first relatively free elections in 52 years the "Socialistic" part of the name is being deleted.

Beside Istra, Croats settled also in various portions of today's Slovenia, as well as in some parts of Northern Italy. These Croats, of course, from the earliest time have intermixed with Italians, often to a point that it was impossible to differentiate among them. Most of them also adopted Italian names. A similar situation arose later in Dalmatia too, in fact almost everywhere along the Adriatic coast. From the 11th to the 14th centuries Venice conquered and possessed, often for extended period, many Croatian coastal cities as well as islands. In 1409, Venice acquired most of Dalmatia and held it until 1797. During this period the influence of Italian language, culture and customs was enormous. Most of the better-off Dalmatian families adopted the Italian language or at least were able enough to use it, and names were regularly Italianized, even in that part of Dalmatia which was not under Venice (Dubrovnik). Dalmatian and other Croats studied in Italy, lived in Italy, settled permanently in Italy often in great number, especially those who fled from the

Turks. In many areas of Italy their presence was particularly strong and noticeable. In Northern Italy, in bordering regions, Croats had lived since the earliest time. Also they were numerous along the Adriatic coast, notably around Ancona and Ravenna. In Loreto, near Ancona, a college for the education of Croatian clergy was founded in the 16th century. The Croats lived (and still live) in Molise, originally an exclusive colony of Croats which was created by Croatian refugees who fled to Italy to escape from Turkish onslaught and occupation. In many villages there the Croatian language is still spoken today. A number of Croats lived also in Apulia, mostly refugees too. The Croats could have been found even in Naples which historically had strong and close ties to Croatia (The Anjouvin House of Naples reigned in Croatia for more than a century).

In Rome an entire area of the city where Croatians lived was called in the Middle Ages "Croatian neighborhood" ("vicolo dei Schiavoni"). It had its own congregation, the center of which was "Collegium Croaticum ad S. Hieronymus" (Croatian College of St. Hieronymus). It still exists today in Rome as the "Croatian Institute of St. Hieronymus". St. Hieronymus, a Roman saint (died in 420), is the patron saint of Dalmatia and by extension of all Croatia. The Croats maintained also close ties with Genoa and were present in Genoa too. For example, in the great war with Venice (1378-1381) the Croats and the Genoese were allies. In 1379, in naval battle near Pula the united Genoese-Croatian fleet consisting of 23 vessels routed the Venetian fleet which lost 15 ships and 2,4000 men.

In this battle the Genoese admiral Luciano Doria was killed but his second-in-command, Ambrosio Doria polished off the Venetians.

In the 15th, 16th and 17th centuries the Croatian ships from Dubrovnik sailed regularly in the service of Genoa. The Genoese preferred to rent them together with all their crews and officers who were highly esteemed in Genoa. In fact, the Genoese studied and used some Croatian navigational techniques developed in Dubrovnik, certainly, the supreme compliment to the skill of Croatian mariners. As the author and navigational expert, Josip Luetić, points out in his book about the ships and mariners from the Republic of Dubrovnik (published in Zagreb in 1984) in the office "Conservatori del Mare" in Genoa frequent references are found about the "navigation in a manner of those from Dubrovnik."

Individually, also, many Croats navigated on Genoese ships in those times. (It is also quite possible that an obscure Croatian soldier of fortune and sailor later known as Christopher Columbus once made a trip or two on the Genoese ships).

A strong Croatian presence existed for a long time also in Bologna. A college for the students from Croatia and Hungary called "Hungaro-Croatian college" ("Collegium Hungarico-Croaticum") was founded there in 1552 and operated without interruption until 1781.

And, of course, most of all, there was Venice. For centuries not only political and administrative center of Adriatic Croats but also, to a considerable extent, Venice was their cultural, social and economic center as well. Venice was always even before, thru the centuries full of Croats and since the acquisition of Dalmatia there were Croatian sailors, soldiers, merchants and residents everywhere. A Croatian fraternal association of Sv. Juraj (St. George) and St. Trifun was founded in Venice in the 15th century—in Columbus time—and existed for four centuries until 1866.[1] Croatian soldiers, the "Cappellatti Croati", mounted guard in the city and Croatian inhabitants regularly congregated on that famous "Riva od Hrvata" ("Riva dei Schiavoni") or "Croatian Coast".[2] On that Croatian Coast the library of Bartolomeo Occhi, which printed Croatian books, was later situated, making Venice literally a mixed Italo-Croatian city. In short, the Croats were more or less at home in Italy which was practically a mixed Italo-Croatian land, at least from the Croatian point of view, taking into consideration that Croatia is relatively a small nation. And vice versa, Dalmatian cities imported from Italy teachers, writers, craftsmen, musicians; the high church hierarchy was mainly Italian and even a number of Italian colonists settled in Dalmatia giving this region also a certain Italian flavor. And there was more to this inter-mixing: While in Rome there was a "Croatian neighborhood" in the Middle Ages, in Zagreb, for example there was in those times an "Italian neighborhood" as well as the Venetian Street in the upper part of town. The most prominent Italian who settled and married in

Zagreb in 14th century (1399) was Niccolo Alighieri the great-grandson of the famous poet Dante Alighieri, the author of "La Divin Comedia." He was the towns pharmacist. Furthermore, there were many Italians elsewhere in Croatia, particularly in Istra.

This must be understood before we tackle the question of Columbus. Due to a historical situation like that, which is poorly known or unknown in the West, many Croats have made a name in Italy or out of Italy—and among them we must include, tentatively, Columbus himself—without the credit ever being given to the country from which they hailed and to a Croatian people to which they really belonged. Due to their usually Italianized names they are automatically taken for Italians, often even by many scholars who do not have sufficient knowledge of Croatian nation and, in particular, the relationship of its people with the Italians. And this must be emphasized strongly: Whenever we find in those times a certain Italian whose family name (its origin) cannot be traced in Italy and whose native place is unknown in Italy there is at least a fifty-fifty chance that this person was originally a Croatian. For example, just to name few notable and most famous cases, Marco Polo for one, the great Venetian traveler and Admiral, the real precursor of Columbus, was of Croatian origin whose family hailed from the Island of Korčula.[3] Croatian was Cardinal Andrea Zamometić called Zuccalmaglio, the real precursor of the Reformation, who convoked the Council of Basel in 1482, and tried unsuccessfully to reform the Catholic church. Croatian was Luciano de Laurana, born in Vrana in Dalmatia (Vrana is Laurana in Italian), generally considered the greatest architect of all times.

Another great architect from the 15th century, Giorgio Dalmata (Juraj Dalmatian), was also Croatian, as was Giulio Clovio (Clovich), often called the "Titian in miniature", a close personal friend of Michelangelo and the greatest miniature painter of all times, who was also Croatian born and on whose tomb in Ravenna in Italy is written that he was "Croata de Croatia".

Croatian was the famous Pope Sixtus V, (1585–1590), who was born in the Croatian colony of Molise in Italy which was formed by Croatian refugees fleeing the Turks and where they still today speak the Croatian language. Croatian was Marco Antonio de

Dominis (Gospodnetić), born on the Island of Rab, the great scientist and philosopher and former Archbishop of Split who died in a Roman prison and whose body was burned, posthumously in 1624, by the Inquisition on Campo del Fiore. (It is said Francis Bacon copied his works). Croatian was the famous sculptor (Stalić), in Italy called Stalio Schiavone (Stalio the Croat). Croatian was the great Renaissance painter Vittorio Carpaccio (Karpač), born in Istra. Croatian were also two other famous painters of the epoch, Andrea Schiavone (Andrija Medulić) and Giorgio Schiavone (Juraj Čulinović). Croatian was the noted mathematician, naturalist and antiquarian Fray Francesco Patrizio Dalmatino (Fr. Franjo Patričić). Croatian was the great musician and composer Giuseppe Tartini (Josip Trtanj). Croatian was also Giovanni Caboto or Cabota (Ivan Cabota), in England known as John Cabot, the famous Venetian mariner, contemporary and very probably an old acquaintance of Columbus. Croatian was also Niccolo Tommaseo (Tomašić), writer and the greatest literary critic of Italy, who was born in Šibenik in Croatia and who also wrote in his native Croatian. And Croatian was, of course, Ruggiero Josip Bošković the father of atomic science.

Yet, because of generally poor knowledge in the West and, especially in America, of Croatian history and the Croatian people and in particular of their historical connections and ethnical ties with Italian people, all those men with their usually Italianized names are automatically assumed to have been Italians.

It was usual, literally inevitable, thru centuries, for a Croatian who found himself in Italy to be taken automatically for an Italian. Perhaps the best example is the case of the mentioned Ruggiero (Ruger) Bošković (1711–1787), the Jesuit priest from Dubrovnik and great scientist and philosopher who is honored as the father of modern atomic science. Though he did not even come from Venetian-owned Dalmatia but from the free Croatian territory of the Republic of Dubrovnik and despite the fact that he was one of those Croats who did not Italianize his name, contrary to the usual custom, he is, nevertheless, with all this considered by Italians, more or less, to have been one of their own and his name adorns the streets of many cities in Italy.

As for the seamanship and naval ties between Croatians and Italians those were also very close and their seamanship was more or less the same. The Croatians were thoroughly a sea-faring nation.

They ranked always, throughout the Middle Ages up to the modern times, as among the most outstanding navigators in Europe. They were equal to Spaniards, Portuguese and Italians. Their seamanship was the same; it was, in reality, an extension of this brilliant Hispano-Italian seamanship which grew out from various factors: Croatian maritime traditions, the common Mediterranean geographical position and above all from the close links, historical, ethnic, cultural, religious, military and naval the Adriatic Croats had with their neighbors and quasi compatriots, the Italians, and with Spain. Croatia's seafaring and naval prowess came into focus early in the 9th century with the emergence in the neighborhood of one powerful rival—Venice. A furious struggle for domination of the Adriatic ensued and lasted for centuries. In fact, for nearly a thousand years, Croatia's history was tied, one way or another, to that of Venice.

Vladislav I (821–830) was the first Croatian ruler to make a short lived peace treaty with the Venetians (In Venice in 829). Mislav (830–845) fought both the Venetians and Franks. King Trpimir I (845–864), one of the most powerful sovereigns of Croatia, defied the Franks and defeated the Byzantines, Bulgarians and Venetians. His fleet once looted Caorle near Venice. His successor, Domagoi (864–876) was forced to fight with almost everybody and was marked in the annals of Venice as the "worst (pessimus) ruler" of the Croats. His son, Branimir (879–892) faced the triple coalition of Franks (Holy Roman Empire), the Byzantine Empire and Venice, but resisted successfully against great odds. He made peace with the Byzantines, repulsed the Franks and then confronted, decisively, the Venetians. In 887 in the great battle near Makarska the Venetian fleet was destroyed. In this battle the Doge of Venice, Peter Candiano, was killed. The Venetians then sued for peace and agreed to pay a yearly tribute to the sovereigns of Croatia in exchange for the right of free navigation in the Adriatic. The Venetians continued to pay this tribute for the next 113 years!

Croatia's naval power came to its zenith during the reign of the King Tomislav (910–929) who repulsed the Bulgarians and the much-feared Hungarians who settled in neighboring Pannonian plains in 896, during the reign of his father, King Muncimir. According to his contemporary, the Byzantine emperor Constantine VII the Porphyrogenitus, Croatia's navy consisted then of 100 sagenas (large warships) and 80 konduras (smaller warships). This was a navy second only to that of the Byzantine Empire in Europe.

But in the second half of the 10th century during the reign of Držislav (969–997) when the Bulgarians conquered and occupied the Eastern part of Croatia, its naval power diminished drastically. This did not escape the keen eye of the Venetian Doge Peter II Orseolo, the greatest Doge in the history of Venice. When in the year 1000, the envoys of Croatian king Svetislav came to Venice to collect the usual tribute the Doge told them that he would go to Croatia and will bring it personally! He did go—with the fleet—conquering many Coratian coastal cities and islands, thus renewing the old struggle which lasted for the next 50 years. King Peter Kresimir IV (1056–1074), whom Croatian historians like to call the Great, reestablished Croatian domination and in one royal diploma called the Adriatic sea "our sea" (mare mostrum). One of his successors, Zvonimir (1076–1089), under Papal urging made a naval alliance with the Normans from South Italy and their leader Robert Guiscard against the Byzantine Empire and Venice. The united Croato-Norman fleet which eventually grew to 120 vessels defeated the Byzantines and the Venetians under Durazzo in 1083 and repeated the same feat the next year in the great battle at Kasope near the Island of Corfu in which the Byzantines and Venetians used the famous "Greek fire" to no avail.

But with the death of king Stephen II (1089–1091) the Croatian national dynasty was extinguished and the country promptly disintegrated. The Byzantines and Venetians occupied most of Dalmatia. In 1102, the Croats elected an Arpadian, the Hungarian King Koloman (a nephew of Zvonimir, by marriage) to be Croatian King. Thus, Hungary and Croatia entered into a personal union (confederation) having the same King but remaining two separate states. The main task of the Arpadians was to recombine the parts of the old Kingdom of the Croats and to boot out the Byzantines and the Venetians, a difficult task they largely accomplished: Koloman (1102–1116), the first of the Arpadians, Stephen III the Thunderbolt (King of Croatis 1108–1116, then of both 1116–1131) Bela I the Blind (1131–1141) and Geissa (1141–1162) fought for decades furiously and incessantly for the Croatian Adriatic littoral and by 1180, during the reign of Bela II the Byzantines and the Venetians were completely ousted from Croatian soil for a long time—the Byzantines, in fact, forever.

In the 14th century, however, during the reign of the new dynasty—the Anjouvins of Naples—Venice seized anew many strongholds in Dalmatia before the ascent to the throne of King Ludovic I the Great (1342–1382). In 1356, he began to assemble a big army in Zagreb telling everyone willing to listen that he was going to conquer the East, but when the army was ready he suddenly turned West declaring a war on the Republic of Venice. The normally astute and well informed Venetians were taken, this time, completely by surprise and after two years of fighting were ousted from Croatian shores.

King Ludovic I reorganized the Croatian naval forces and established the post of the Admiral of Croatia (admiratus regnorum Dalmatiae et Croatiae). He had his seat in Zadar. With him there was also the Vice-admiral.

In the second war which started in 1378 and in which Genoa was an ally of the Croats, the Venetians were again beaten and by the treaty of Turin in 1381 were obliged to pay to the Hungaro-Croatian kings a yearly tribute of 7,000 gold ducats. It was something like in the old times during the reign of the Croatian national dynasty. But, after the death of Ludovic I the Croatians plunged into a 25-year long civil war in which at one point—in 1390—they had four kings: Maria, the daughter and the successor of Ludovic I, Sigismund (Luxemburg) her husband, Tvrdko I, once the local Ban of Bosnia who proclaimed himself King of Bosnia in 1377 and then of all Croatia, and Ladislaus IV of Naples, the last Anjouvin. The contest eventually narrowed to two: Ladislaus of Naples and Sigismund. The great majority of Croats favored the Neapolitan and in 1403, the leader of the Croats, Hrvoje Vukčić-Hrvatinić, the Grand Duke of Bosnia, brought Ladislaus to Croatia and had him crowned in Zadar. But he was afraid to go to Hungary where his father was murdered in 1386 and soon returned to Naples, leaving the Duke Hrvatinić as his regent in Croatia. The Duke defended the country successfully against the rival Sigismund until 1408 when Sigismund, under the pretext of fighting the "heretics" among the Croats, organized an international crusade. In 1408, in a battle near Dobor in Bosnia, the Croats, led by the young king Tvrdko II of Bosnia, were defeated and forced to bow to Sigismund. Nevertheless, many cities and islands in Dalmatia continued, even after this defeat, to recognize Ladislaus of Naples as their king. But his cause was finished. Therefore he entered into secret negotiations with Venice and, in 1409, sold to the Venetians "his rights" to Dalmatia for 100,000 gold ducats! After this shameful act of Ladislaus', Venice immediately began to conquer Croatian cities and islands in Dalmatia claiming she bought it from the "legitimate king"!

The King Sigismund, now the undisputed sovereign of the Croats, was unable to prevent it despite the fact that he led three consecutive wars for Dalmatia. Besides, there appeared another, far greater peril: the Turks, which by this time had already conquered most of the Balkans. Shortly afterwards almost everyone was fighting for his own survival. So the question of Dalmatia became secondary and Venice was left in possession of most of it until her end in 1797. At that time she was replaced by the Hapsburg Monarchy of which Croatia was now a part.

It should be noted that the mutual sentiments between the Venetians and the Croats, even before Venice acquired Dalmatia and some other parts, generally were, surprisingly, friendly (at least between the wars). It was that peculiar kind of relationship the Croats had with all other Italians. Even centuries before Venice gained most of Dalmatia, the intermixing between Venetians and Croats was frequent and many Croats settled in Venice. One of those earlier settlers in Venice was the famous family Polo (Polić) in the 13th century. That extraordinary Croato-Venetian relationship, as it can be ascertained now, played no small role in the events which eventually led to the discovery of America. Today it seems certain that Venice was the starting point in the career of Christopher Columbus, just as it was for that of John Cabot. That relationship, of course, also had a strong impact on Venice's own maritime activities and naval strength.

Thru the centuries, and particularly after 1409, when Venice gained most of Dalmatia and held it until 1797, Venetians used Croatian seamen in massive numbers. Especially after 1409, they became the backbone of Venetian naval power: the Venetian fleet was almost literally a Croatian fleet. The crews of Venetian warships were always overwhelmingly composed of Croats.[4]

Venice, in fact, owed almost all its maritime glory to her Croats. In recognition of this service the flagship of the Venetian admiral carried twelve chosen Croatian flagbearers. Not only the low personnel, but officers too were in great number Croatian and often occupied even the top positions. For example, a Croatian (Vid Mazarević) commanded the most famous Venetian warship of the 17th century: the "Giove Fulminate".

And besides all those ties with Italians and Italy the Croats also had strong ties thru the centuries with Spain, too. After the loss of most of Dalmatia to Venice the center of Croatian maritime activities became South Dalmatia which was not taken by Venice, but remained an integral part of the Kingdom of Croatia. There was the famous City of Dubrovnik (Ragusa), an autonomous Croatian city-republic, similar to Venice and Genoa.

Venetian nobleman Zoane Battista Giustiniani said this, in 1553, about the maritime prosperity of Dubrovnik: "There are many heads of families who have a fortune of hundred thousands of (gold) ducats and more and they navigate in all regions of the globe and have in all one hundred large ships, smaller sailships numbering about 50, and about 5,000 seamen."

Bartolomeo Crescenzio, author of the book "Nautica Mediterranea" (published in Rome in 1607), the most referred-to and cited by naval experts says: "Of all experts and masters for galleons the most numerous and probably the most capable in this (Mediterranean) sea are those from Dubrovnik". Another Italian, Pantero Pantera in his book "L'armata navale" (1614), describing various types of ships says: "The navas (naos) from Dubrovnik are the biggest and most esteemed by all". Of the sea power of Dubrovnik the local noted navigator, Marin Sagri-Krivonosić said: "We know that almost one hundred ships from Dubrovnik are cutting the seas in all four corners of the world." In a letter from 1634, which is conserved in the archives of the city of Dubrovnik, Spanish admiral Andrija Ohmučević-Grgurić, (a Croatian) among other says this for Dubrovnik: "In the past, as it is well known, there were 70–80 navas and large ships in this glorious Republic . . . which were named by 5,000 persons."[5]

The Croats did not only navigate for their own account and in the service of Venice, Genoa and Spain. Croatian mariners served also in other European countries including France and England. John Cabot (Giovanni Caboto) undoubtedly a Croatian mariner from Dalmatia, discovered for England parts of North America in 1497. This Croat was a forerunner of the English Empire in America. In his second voyage to the New World he was accompanied by numerous Croats from Venetian Dalmatia.[6]

Of course, the Islamized Croats played also great role in the history of the naval forces of the Ottoman Empire. Numerous Croats were Turkish admirals. Some of them were even noted pirates before becoming admirals, like the famous Dragut, for example, and such a career was not strange to Christopher Columbus who similarly rose from a pirate to a great admiral! Several Croats held the position of "Kapudan-pasha" (First admiral) of Turkish Empire.

And when the young Russian czar Peter the Great decided to modernize his backward and semi-Asiatic country, to whom else would he turn to teach his people navigation and to build Russia's first navy, but to the Croats of South Dalmatia whose skill, seamanship and great maritime traditions were known all over Europe. Croatian captains and experts from Boka Kotorska built and organized the first Russian navy on the Baltic and a Croatian, Matija Zmajević, became the first admiral in the history of Russia. He defeated the Swedes in three naval battles in the Baltic Sea. A Croatian naval expert and mathematician Marko Martinović, recommended by Venice to Peter the Great, founded the first Russian naval academy. The Croats from South Dalmatia were also the principal founders of Russian Black Sea fleet in which the main roles were played by members of the Croatian aristocratic family of Count Vojnović from Perast in Boka Kotorska.

And when in 1797, Venice disappeared and Dalmatia by the treaty of Campo Formio was taken over by Francis II, and incorporated into the Hapsburg Monarchy (the Emperor Francis II took over Dalmatia in his quality as a King of Hungary and Croatia), the Croats were the ones, naturally, who built the

Monarchy's sea power, for almost the entire coast belonging to Hapsburgs was Croatian, the ships were built in Croatian ship-yards by Croatian experts and workers, were manned by Croatian crew and the officer's corps was always predominantly Croatian (despite certain discrimination in favor of Germans and Hungarians, of course, when the top positions in the navy were concerned).

The Monarchy's splendid naval victory over Italy near Vis (Lissa) in 1866 was the feat of Croatian sailors, so was the famous Polar expedition of Payer and Weyprecht in 1873, with the ship "Tegethof" (Croatian crew) in which the Land of Francis Joseph was discovered. And, of course, the Monarchy's merchant marine was for most part a private Croatian property. The most notable example was the famous Cosulich (Kožulić) family from Trieste (Cosulich Line) which was ranked among the biggest shipowners in the world prior to 1914. The family is still in business today in Italy. (Trieste is today in Italy).

With such seafaring traditions and, especially, with such close ties with Italians and Spaniards it should really not be a great surprise if the once an obscure mariner called today Christopher Columbus turns out to have been a certain Croatian.

What we are really dealing with here is the case of one so far unknown Croatian adventurer and soldier of fortune who came to Spain and Portugal by the usual way of Italy and who, in 1484, on the Portuguese island of Madeira, learned about the existence of the lands across the ocean which were discovered by chance by certain Spanish pilot, Alonso Sanchez de Huelva. Christopher Columbus simply kept the secret of this discovery for himself. The rest is history.[7]

All confusion about Columbus' real identity, national origin, past life and experience was in fact deliberately created by Columbus himself so that he alone could benefit from this secret and collect all the glory.

But despite taking extraordinary care and precautions to cover all possible tracks by which he succeeded, more or less, in fooling us all for five centuries, the real Columbus can now be unmasked and the truth about the real discovery, that of 1484, can now be accepted. This is important for historic reasons as well as for the reason of simple justice, especially now when we are going soon to celebrate the half-millenium of the official discovery of America. I believe it is about time that this great historical hoax be put in proper perspective and credits given where credits belonged. This does not necessarily mean that Columbus himself has no historical merits whatsoever (after all the new history begins with him, like it or not), but the truth about the discovery must be established. The truth about the real Columbus, Columbus the person, must be also established. Although it is impossible from the meager data we have on him to ascertain his personal identity, however, thru a careful and detailed study his national origin—that of one Croatian soldier of fortune—can now be established, I believe, almost with certainty.

To be more precise: There is nothing of what we know for sure about Columbus today that cannot be connected and squared with this Croatian background. Every known fact fits in. The cumulative evidence is overwhelming:

1. The Croats had close ties with Spain for centuries going back all the way to Moorish Spain. In Columbus' time and in the subsequent era of the great discoveries those ties were not just close—they were special and in many aspects unique in history. Many factors contributed to this principal including, of course, geographical and historical. Both Croatia and Spain were part of the Mediterranean and both had extraordinary ties to Italy which was sort of a bridge between the two countries thru which all the traffic from Croatian lands passed on its way to Spain. Those ties were developed especially thru the Kingdom of Naples to which both the Croats and the Spaniards, particularly the Aragonese, were closely linked. The Croats brought Carlo Roberto of the House of Naples (the Anjou dynasty) to Croatia in 1300. The House of Naples reigned in Croatia from 1301 to 1409, and in the allied Kingdom of Hungary from 1302 to 1395.

The ties between the Croats and Spaniards became direct and even closer when the Spanish (Aragonese) dynasty came to the throne of Naples in 1443. The Aragonese dynasty, as the successor of the Anjouvins, immediately laid claim to the throne of Hungary and Croatia as well. There was no chance for the Aragonese in Hungary, but in Croatia, situated along the shores of Adriatic and having a direct sea link to Naples, they had more luck. Alfonso V, the Magnanimous the king of Aragon and Naples actually succeeded in becoming at least a partial sovereign of the Croats (1445-1458). A large part of Dalmatia and the Duchy of Hum (Herzegovina) recognized him as their lawful king. It is entirely possible, in fact very likely, that an unknown young Croatian soldier of fortune, later known as Cristobal Colon (Christopher Columbus), after some wandering thru Italy came to Naples in 1450's during the reign of Alfonso V. From some of Columbus' letters it is clear that he knew Naples very well. It seems that after the death of Alfonso he took part in the civil war which erupted there for the succession of the throne between Ferrante the illegitimate son of Alfonso V, and French pretender Renato (René) of Anjou. According to Columbus himself he took the side of Renato before returning to the service of Aragon and later of Castile too. (Spain became an unified country in 1469, after the marriage of Ferdinand of Aragon and Isabella of Castile). "I came to serve at age of twenty-eight"—Columbus wrote later to the sovereigns of Spain. (That's when and how he learned Spanish).

As a matter of fact the ties between the Croats and Spain reached their peak and were the closest during the lifetime of Christopher Columbus. The emotional, cultural, religious, maritime and national ties in general were very close, particularly between the Croats from South Dalmatia and Spain. Croatian mariners served on Spanish ships, Croatian ships navigated in service of Spain, Croatian soldiers served in the Spanish army, Croatian students studied in Salamanca (the "Salamankezi" as they were called in Dalmatia). In Columbus' time Spain exercised great influence in South Dalmatia which left permanent traces in many aspects of the life, culture and customs of South Dalmatian Croats. Some of these still exist in our time like, for example, the famous chivalric play "Moresca" on the Island of Korčula which was brought from Columbus' Spain by the Islanders taken to Spain by the fleet of Frederic of Aragon.

In Columbus' time also the church of Spain, especially thru the person of Cardinal Juan de Torquemada, was the main actor in the fight against the Patharenic-Manichean heresy among the Croats and contributed much to the conversion and reincorporation of the Manicheans back into Catholic church.

In the same time even family ties developed among the Royal house of Spain and the leading Croatian family, that of Frankopan. Prince Bernardin Frankopan the principal magnate of the Kingdom of Croatia married Spanish princess Luisa of Aragon niece of King Ferdinand. Their son, named Christopher (born in 1482), became a great name in Croatian history—a Ban (Viceroy) of Croatia and a national hero.

In 1470, Dubrovnik, already closely linked to Spain, was granted special prileges by Spanish king Ferdinand by which it could trade freely in his Kingdom of Naples. In 1507, those were enlarged by the same king Ferdinand who confirmed in a royal decree all previous privileges, enumerated in 26 paragraphs, which Dubrovnik enjoyed in Naples and all those privileges were now extended throughout the Spanish Empire. The decree gave to this Croatian city an extraordinary and special status within the lands of Spanish crown all around the world and contributed the most to the three centuries of close ties between Dubrovnik and Spain.

From the onset the ships from Dubrovnik were the only other authorized ships, the only other ships beside the Spanish ones, which sailed to New World. Those were the glory days when Dubrovnik reached its zenith primarily thanks to its fabulous "Spanish connection". Dubrovnik was, then, probably the most prosperous city in Europe. In the English language to this day we use the word "Argosy" which in those times denoted a perfectly built ship from Dubrovnik with rich cargo. "Argosy" comes from "Aragosa" or "Arragouse" which means Ragusa or Dubrovnik (Even Shakespeare talks about the "Argosy" in two of his plays). The ships from Dubrovnik navigated all the known routes of the Mediterranean and the Atlantic, the seamen from Dubrovnik were famous everywhere and its shipbuilding industry was rated one of the best in the world. Or as the old Croatian poet and writer from Dubrovnik, Mauro Vetranović, a contemporary of Columbus said: "Dubrovnik whose glory thru the world resounds and particularly where the Croatian language is found".

In the 15th, 16th and 17th centuries, in fact, most of the Croatian ships from Dubrovnik were at one time or another in the service of Spain. Croatian mariners from Dubrovnik participated also in Columbus' voyages to New World.[8] It is believed that even on the very first voyage of discovery as many as three Croatian sailors from Dubrovnik took part (under Spanish names) and that two of them returned to tell the story.[9] (It was customary for the Croats in those times to change or refashion their names depending on the country in which they lived or served). Two of those three probably had the name, Martolosić (Martolosich).

Interestingly enough it is now believed that a certain sailor in Columbus' expedition called Fernandez, who achieved the dubious distinction of being the first European to have been killed by Indians had in reality a name like Martolosich. It is also interesting to note that from this Slavic name some Poles have concluded that this Martolosich was probably a Pole and by extension assumed that Columbus himself may have been too! Unfortunately for the Poles this Martolosich had nothing to do with Poland. The family Martolosić whose members took part in the discovery is a well known and noble Croatian family, known before Columbus and after Columbus. The family comes from the Island of Lopud, near Dubrovnik, and has been from Columbus' time on thru generations in the service of Spain to which it gave several pilots, captains and even admirals. The best one known, Christopher Martolosić, in a testament made in Naples in 1628 and registered in Dubrovnik in 1635, gives himself the title of governor (admiral) of one Spanish squadron of "galleons in Ocean". This is also mentioned by the Italian writer Francesco Appendini who lived in Dubrovnik and who said that the members of the Martolosić family participated in the discovery of new lands in America. In some local sources there is also mention that in 1493, the Archbishop of Dubrovnik wrote a letter to Pope Alexander VI, (a Spaniard) in which he informed the Pontiff about the adventures of two sailors from Dubrovnik who were with Columbus on his first voyage.[10]

It was also natural that the Croats who sailed first with the Spaniards to New World, both, individually on Spanish ships as well as collectively on Croatian ships from Dubrovnik in the service of Spain, were also the first, beside the Spaniards, to come and settle in the New World. They began to arrive even before the conquest of American mainland started. Among the first steady settlers known were Mato Konkegjević and his brother Dominik in 1520. Both were from the Island of Lopud near Dubrovnik, the same island from which also hailed the members of Martolosić family who were with Columbus in the discovery. They spent about 30 years in Indias, that is in America, amassed some fortune of 12,000 gold ducats and then unfortunately decided to return to Dubrovnik. They had bad luck: On their return they were attacked and captured near the Spanish coast by French pirates. The Croats came to Mexico during the celebrated conquest by Hernando Cortez. They also came among the first to South America during the equally famous conquest of Peru by another great Spanish conquistador, Francisco Pizarro. It is known from his own testament made in 1589 that a certain Croatian from Dubrovnik, Marin Pincetić, was living in Potosi,the "Silver city" of Peru, probably since the days of the conquest in 1532 (in any case before 1537). In that year—1537—another Croat from Dubrovnik, Basilio Basiljević arrived. In the 16th century numerous Croats lived in the Spanish New World. Many of them remained there for good, some returned home, while many others retired to Spain. Several of them lived and died in Seville as can be seen from the letter which the government of Dubrovnik sent to its envoy in Spain, Orsat Crijević-Tubero in which it tells him that there are sizeable sums of money deposited in Seville from various people from Dubrovnik who were in Indias (America) and died either there or in Seville. It instructs him to contact the Spanish king Phillip II, and kindly ask the King that this money be delivered to the city of Dubrovnik so that it can be distributed among the rightful relatives and heirs.[11]

Among those earlier arrivals to America the most famous was Vincent Spalatin a native of the Island of Korčula who came to Santo Domingo and then Mexico in 1530. He was a Dominican friar and missionary. But beside being a missionary he was a man of many talents and intellectual versatility: a writer, historian, linquist, scientist, educator, administrator, explorer, navigator, superb cartographer and even an expert in land warfare. He translated from Spanish to Italian the book "Dell' Arte del Navigare" ("The Art of Navigation") whose original is preserved today in the Library of the University of Zagreb in Croatia. He made a geographical map of Spain which was recognized as the best of its time. The original map is preserved today in the Museo Correr in Venice. Above all he was an expert on New Spain (North America) and wrote numerous books about it, the most important of which was his book in Latin "De iure belli contra infideles Indiae Occidentalis" ("The Wars against the Infidels of Western Indies") which was dedicated to the Spanish King Phillip II. One of the best cartographers of those times was another Croat, Vincent Volčić (Voltius) born in Dubrovnik. In 1592 he founded the noted school of cartography in Livorno, Italy. A few years later he moved to Naples into Spanish service. One of his famous maps from this period is found today in possession of the Hispanic Society of the U.S.A.

In 1535, warships from Dubrovnik (its entire fleet) participated in the expedition of Spanish king and emperor Charles V, to Tunis in which 18 large galleons from Dubrovnik were lost, complete with their crew.

In 1538, Croatian ships from Dubrovnik participated also in the Battle near Santa Maria de Leuca in which the Turkish fleet, commanded by Hairedin Barbarossa, defeated the Christian fleet (The Holy League) of Spain and Venice. Beside the ships from Dubrovnik in battle also took part the ships from Croatian cities and communes in Venetian-owned Dalmatia—some 25 warships and cargo ships. For a short time a part of South Dalmatia even belonged to Spain when the famous Spanish admiral, Andrea Doria (a Genoese) with the assistance of Croats liberated Herceg-Novi in Boka Kotorska from the Turks. The famous (and infamous) ex-Algerian pirate, Hairedin Barbarossa, soon put an end to it and returned the city to the Turks in 1539, by overwhelming the Spanish-Croatian defenses by sheer numbers in the most desperate struggle the Adriatic probably has ever seen. In horrifying attacks the Turks sometime lost thousands of men in a single night on the streets of Herceg-Novi. All 4,000 defenders died.

In 1541, the ships from Dubrovnik participated again in Spanish expedition of Charles V to Algiers and again sustained heavy losses. In a storm which hit the Spanish armada eight galleons from Dubrovnik sunk. Six more were lost under Tripoli. (Interestingly, weather was never kind to Spaniards throughout history and it was principally the bad weather which ultimately defeated Spain and changed history).

Seven Croatian ships from Dubrovnik also took part in the Spanish expedition of Andrea Doria to Koron.

In the most famous naval battle in history, that of Lepanto in 1571, in which the Turkish might on sea was broken, Croatian vessels from Dubrovnik participated again in coalition with Spanish and Venetian. And, of course, both the Spanish and especially the Venetian fleet had a great number of Croatian seamen and officers aboard. Furthermore, Dalmatian cities and islands also took part by sending their own ships which fought as part of the Venetian fleet. Eleven galleons went to the battle. The names of some of those vessels and of their commanders are known. They were: galleon from the Island of Hvar, "St. Jerolim" or "St. Hieronymous" (Capt. Ivan Balci), galleon from the Island of Krk "Uskrsnuli Krist" (Capt. Ljudevit Cikota), galleon from the Island of Rab, "St. Ivan" (Capt.Ivan Gospodnetić-De Dominis), galleon from the city of Kotor "St. Trifun" (Capt. Jeronim Bizantio), galleon from the city of Trogir, "La Donna" (Capt. Lujo Cippico), galleon from the island of Cres, "St. Nikola" (Capt. Kolan Dražić) and galleon from the city of Kopar, "Il Leone" (Capt. Dominik del Tacco) All fought at Lepanto.[12]

One who particularly excelled in Spanish service thru the most of 16th century was Miho Pracat-Pracatović (1522–1607), a Croatian nobleman and navigator from Dubrovnik who was also one of the biggest shipowners of his time as well as an international merchant and banker. He built, single-handedly, one of the greatest fortunes in Europe—over 200,000 gold ducats—and left it all to his native city for good causes. Miho Pracat-Pracatović was one of the most influential Croats in Spain in his time. The city of Dubrovnik accorded him a special honor: In 1638, a bronze bust of Pracatović was erected in the atrium of the Prince's Palace in Dubrovnik. He was the only citizen in history to be accorded such an honor. Another famous son of Dubrovnik, who excelled in Spanish service was Nikola Sagri-Krivonosić. He was the first one who wrote a book about the ocean currents of the Atlantic. His brother, also a noted shipowner and navigator, Marin Sagri-Krivonosić, had Spanish connections too. As a matter of fact, almost anybody in Dubrovnik who was ever engaged in navigation in the 15th, 16th or 17th century was at some time or other in the service of Spain. For the people of Dubrovnik Spain meant almost as much as their own country and often all of Dubrovnik was in the service of Spain and fought on the side of Spain whenever called on and with all it had. The people of Dubrovnik did that at great peril for their own freedom and well being, especially after 1526, when most of the Kingdom of Croatia was conquered by the Turks and Dubrovnik lost all territorial continuity with what was left of Croatia and found itself completely surrounded by the Turks. But the rulers of Dubrovnik, skillful diplomats that they were, managed to perform maybe the most extraordinary balancing act in history: They battled the Turks on sea in alliance with Spain every time Spain called on them while in the same time officially recognizing (after 1526) the supreme sovereignty of the Sultan and paying Turkey 12,500 gold ducats in yearly tribute! They had it both ways: They conserved their cherished freedom vis-a-vis the Turks and at the same time conserved their cherished ties with Spain, Turkey's main Christian enemy. This is called diplomacy! In those times Spain occupied a special place in the hearts of Adriatic Croats. Spain was always their preferred country (and remains so, to a large extent, even today.)

This explains why Columbus also had a clear preference for Spain and love for Spain above everything else.

Near Dubrovnik lies the old historical town of Slano also known for its Spanish connections. It is a hometown of a famous Croatian family, Ohmučević-Grgurić, which in three generations gave three admirals to Spain. The best known is Petar Ohmučević-Grgurić from the second part of the 16th century who entered the Spanish service with two ships of his own and quickly rose. He became the most famous admiral in Spain when he organized and commanded a small Spanish fleet of twelve chosen ships, all from Dubrovnik—Spanish king Phillip II, called them the "Twelve Apostles"—with whom he won numerous battles against the marauding English fleet. He participated in the unfortunate sailing of the "Invincible Armada" to England in 1588, in which most of the Spanish ships were blown away (as usual) mainly by stormy weather. He continued to battle the English for many years after the defeat of the Armada. His nephew,

Andrija, was also a Spanish admiral. Petar Ohmučević later became the supreme commander of the Spanish Armada, while another Croat, Stjepan Olisti-Tasovčić was the principal aide of the previous commander the Duke of Medina Sidonia who led the Armada in 1588. (Numerous Croatian ships from Dubrovnik took part in that Armada too). His two brothers, Juraj and Petar were also Spanish admirals and were made counts in Spain. Those two renowned Croatian families, Ohmučević-Grgurić and Olisti-Tasovčić, both from Slano, produced among themselves six Spanish admirals, about dozen of captains and some diplomats too. One, another Petar Ohmučević was even consul of Spain in his native Dubrovnik! So, much they were esteemed and trusted in Spain.

Furthermore, from the historic small Island of Lopud near Dubrovnik—the "Isle of the Discoverers"—the members of the noble family, Buna in Spanish service excelled especially. The most famous of them, Vincent Buna (1559–1612), navigated in "both Worlds" as can be read on his tombstone in the Church of St. Trinity on Lopud. That is he was in East India (Goa) as well as in the West (America). Beside being a skillful navigator he was also a diplomat, administrator and statesman of great stature, highly appreciated in the Court of Spain. In fact, he was the second Croat (after Columbus) who achieved the highest possible honor in Spain by ascending to viceroyalty. He was named by the Spanish Crown the Viceroy of Mexico.

In those times also the members of another Croatian family from Dubrovnik, those of Mažibradić, rose in the service of Spain. They had been recommended to the Court of Spain by still another Croatian navigator and shipowner, Thomas Jakoević, native of the Island of Šipan, who was also in the service of Spain with all his ships. Its most well-known member, Jerolim Mažibradić, was a Spanish admiral in 17th century. His illegitimate son, Ivan, was a Spanish governor somewhere in America. The Mažibradić family was an highly gifted, ordinary plebeian family from Dubrovnik which earned its entry into the high nobility of Spain. Its fame began with another Ivan Mažibradić, father of Jerolim, who rose in Spanish service to an admiral and was given a marquisate. His four sons were all in Spanish service. Beside Jerolim two other, Lovro and Nikola were also Spanish admirals and were made counts in Spain. Furthermore, another member of this family, Marin Mažibradić was also Spanish admiral. Thus this family alone, gave five admirals to Spain! Somewhat later, another Croat, Vincent Despotović, became a Spanish viceroy in America, the third one starting with Columbus (or the fourth one if we include Columbus' son, Diego).

With such extraordinary and special relations the Croats had with Spain thru centuries and, especially, in Columbus' time, with so many Croats attaining such great honors in Spain and with other Croats, thousands, indeed tens of thousands of lesser known or unknown ones who were in Spain or in the service of Spain at one time or another and many of whom died fighting with Spain or for Spain the question arises by itself: Was the enigmatic and secretive Christopher Columbus also one of them?

Coupling that with the unique ties the Croats had throughout the history with their neighbors, the Italians, the answer, based for a time being just on that, has to be: It is possible!

After all, what can one typically Croatian-looking, red-haired, blue-eyed man, who refashions his name from country to country as Croatians customarily used to do in those times and who comes to Spain and Portugal from Italy, but does not speak Italian too well be if not a Croat from Dalmatia or some place around along the Croatian Adriatic?

2. Christopher Columbus, the one who officially discovered America as it was previously pointed out most probably did not have anything to do with Genoa except maybe a passing acquaintance. Numerous indications including a statement by Columbus himself show instead that he came originally from Venice or thru Venice, most likely from the Venetian owned Dalmatia which would make Columbus in reality a somewhat Italianized Croat. From some of his writing it is obvious that Columbus knew Venice and the Adriatic—a crucial factor. Naturally, in the controversy which ensued in our century about the real origin of the discoverer of America, Venice, too, was one of the many cities which also claimed the honor of being the birth-place of Columbus. Too bad this claim was not pursued with enough vigor and imagination. They searched for clues in Venice and came up with nothing substantial. But they committed a cardinal error: They omitted to look for clues in the

Venetian-owned shores of North Adriatic, the Croatian-populated Adriatic coast of Istria the islands of Primorje and Dalmatia. Apparently, nobody thought of it.

In those few documents which are left from Columbus and which are unquestionably authentic, the official discoverer of America on several occasions mentions Venice and Venetians. It is interesting and significant to note that Columbus was totally indifferent toward the Genoese and, in fact, on two known occasions fought against Genoa, while for Venice and Venetians he had only sympathy and fondness. This is quite strange for one who is supposed to be Genoese for Venice was thru centuries, as is well known, the perpetual rival and enemy of Genoa.

On the other hand, Christopher Columbus' sympathetic feeling toward Venice is a distinguished mark of a Dalmatian Croat and that same trait—the love for Venice—is found also in another Croat and Columbus' contemporary John Cabot who was only a naturalized citizen of Venice.

Columbus obviously knew Venice. When he discovered the Gulf of Paria (the Northern part of South America), he thought immediately of the "Queen of Adriatic" and of Venetians: the lagoons of the Gulf of Paria reminded him of Venice and the clam fishing of the Indians reminded him of Venetians and their own clam fishing industry. Eventually, this part of America became known as Venezuela ("Little Venice") as Columbus saw it. Commenting on Indian clam fishing Columbus noted the following, as Las Casas marked: " . . . and there are certain roots of trees in the sea which in the language of Hispaniola are called mangles and are full of infinite numbers of clams . . . which are white from inside and very tasty not salty but sweet and need some salt added and he says it is not known where those clams are born, but wherever they are born, they are—says the Admiral—the finest, and they prepare them in the same way as they do in Venice".[13] This note of Columbus proves beyond any doubt that he knew Venice very well. The fact that he knew even the process by which the clams were prepared there testifies that he spent certain period of time as a resident of Venice. Thus, the Republic of St. Mark was the starting point of the great adventure of Christopher Columbus. The remark about Venice, made by Columbus himself, seemingly destroys the notion that the official discoverer of the New World was a Genoese wool-weaver named Christoforo Colombo. That one was never in Venice . . .

3. The Venetian-Croatian origin of Columbus is further indicated by another episode in his life: his great friendship with the young Venetian diplomat Angelo Trivigiano in 1501. Trivigiano was the secretary of the Venetian legation in Spain. His meeting with Columbus resulted in an immediate friendship between the two men. Of his great friendship with the discoverer (a gran amicizia cum a Columbo) Trivigiano reported home to the famous Venetian admiral Domenico Malipiero. He asked Trivigiano to obtain from Columbus the log of his voyages as well as a nautical chart. In what is most surprising, Columbus acceded to the demand of his Venetian friend quickly, and without any questioning or reluctance furnished to Trivigiano even more documents then he wished including copies of many of his letters about the discovery which he wrote to the King and Queen of Spain. Columbus even sent for a map of discovery, which was in Granada, to be delivered to Trivigiano. What Columbus was really doing was giving away to Venice the things which were considered the secrets of the state of Spain!

Why Columbus was so eager and willing to furnish the details of his discovery and a nautical chart to the Republic of St. Mark? How could the alleged Genoese have such friendly feeling toward the Venetians and love for Venice the perennial rival and enemy of Genoa? (Columbus never gave anything to Genoa!)

Obviously he could not have had his pro-Venetian sentiments if he was not a Croat from Dalmatia. To prove this particular point we have to examine, shortly, the rule of Venice over Croatian Dalmatia.

The Republic of St. Mark had fought for centuries for Dalmatian cities and islands with variable fortune, and when in the beginning of the 15th century most of this part of Adriatic Croatia was definitively acquired, Venice was very careful and considerate in her handling of the recently obtained Dalmatia. The Venetians avoided any unpopular measures to not cause discontent among the Dalmatian Croats. Of course Venice profited economically from the acquisition of Dalmatia thru various means, like, for example, the trade monopoly (Dalmatian Croats were obliged to export their products only to Venice and import only from Venice), but otherwise, Venice did not burden them with any excessive obligations. The taxes were very small, often non-existent. Venice respected the customs, the way of life and traditional laws of the Croats. Dalmatian communities, cities, villages and counties remained more or less governed according to their old and own local Croatian laws, constitutions, statutes and privileges in their own Croatian language. Venetians even periodically inquired and consulted with authorities of Free Croatia about the customs and traditional laws of the Croats so that they could better administer Dalmatia according to the habitual traditions of her people.

Venetian authorities in Dalmatia even adopted and used that Greco-Croatian alphabet, the Bosnian-Croatian alphabet which was used in some parts of Dalmatia to make it easier for the local population. Venice, equally, did not touch the national sentiments of Dalmation Croats. During the Venetian rule in Dalmatia (1409-1797) modern nationalism (and chauvinism) had not yet run wild in Europe like it did in the 19th century and after. Thus the Venetian period was also the golden period of Croatian culture in Dalmatia. Many of the greatest works in Croatian literature were written in Venetian Dalmatia as well as some of the greatest and basic works on Croatian history, and most of the books in the Croatian language were printed and published in City of Venice itself, which was thus not only the political center of Dalmatian Croats but also their cultural center as well.

The subject of Croatian culture in Venetian Dalmatia is, of course, a lengthy subject. It would take an entire book to review all the patriotic works of Dalmatian Croats which were written and published during Venetian rule which of course cannot be done here, and it is not necessary for this is a fact so widely known.[14] The main point is that Venetian rule in Dalmatia was generally good and was popular among Dalmatian Croats. The Republic of St. Mark was popular in Dalmatia to such an extent that one can almost say that Dalmatian Croats, in general, loved Venice more then Venetian-Italians did themselves. And the Republic of St. Mark rested mainly on the shoulders of her Croats. Dalmatian Croats usually from the islands served in

Venetian navy, they always made up the enormous majority of Venetian naval personnel and were mostly volunteers. The Croatian land army in Venice numbered up to 60,000 soldiers, almost all volunteers.[15] The Croatian soldiers in Venice were just that—Croatian soldiers; their officers and men used their own Croatian language and were even usually dressed in their own national uniforms . . .

Hence, when Venice was threatened in 1796–1797 by the invading French troops of Napoleon Bonaparte, the Venetians were not the ones who were willing to fight for their Republic and their freedom. Such sacrifice only the Croats from Dalmatia were willing to make. The then liberal Venetian establishment from the period of Enlightenment was ready to yield to the French and dissolve the Republic, but the Dalmatians as one rose up to defend the "Serenissimo Doge of Venice" against the French "apostates and Jacobins". Whoever was able to stand on his feet volunteered to go to defend the Republic, putting the Venetian governor of Dalmatia in an embarrassing position for he had only arms, ammunition and enough ships for transportation for 40,000 men. Those 40,000 Croatian boys were sent to Venice burning from the desire to cross their sabers with Frenchmen, but the degenerate city capitulated without a fight, and furious and chagrined Croatian warriors were dispatched home.

When the sad news of the fall of Venice reached Dalmatia riots resulted; the mob ran wild in several cities of Dalmatia seizing and lynching some notable persons which were known for their links with liberal Venetian establishment of Enlightenment and were sympathetic for the new revolutionary ideas. Out of sheer despair and disappointment the mob accused them of being culpable for the fall of the beloved Republic of St. Mark!—The riots only subsided when the Austrian, de facto, Croatian army commanded by Croatian general Baron Mato Rukavina entered the country and announced to the population that it was taking over in the name of the King of Hungary and Croatia.[16]

These were then the general sentiments of Dalmatian Croats toward Venice and those sentiments help to explain why both, Christopher Columbus and John Cabot, though neither of them Venetian-born, possessed an unquestionable love for Venice.

Their love for Venice betrays thee Croatians in them . . . To summarize: There are three facts which are known about Christopher Columbus. These are the following:

a) Christopher Columbus knew Venice and resided for a certain period in Venice.

b) Christopher Columbus' attitude toward Venice and Venetians is that of sympathy and love.

c) Christopher Columbus did not speak Italian well and the origin of his family cannot be traced on the Italian side of Venice.

From these arguments follow the potential and fairly logical conclusion: Christopher Columbus was a Dalmatian Croat who hailed either from Venetian-owned Dalmatia or from that part of South Dalmatia (Dubrovnik and its surroundings) which then belonged to the Kingdom of Croatia.

Taking into consideration the fact that Columbus definitively knew Venice one can hardly see any other alternative to such a conclusion. And starting from the point that he came thru Venice, his Croatian origin comes to light thru numerous and often very convincing indications.

4. One such indication for the Croatian origin of Columbus is indirectly supplied by Bartolome de Las Casas himself in his "Historia de las Indias" in which he gave a vague description of the original country of Columbus' brothers. And those notation of Las Casas have been baffling historians, both Spanish and Italian, to this day. After saying, with his usual reserve, that nobody knows the name of the place where Columbus was born, Las Casas adds affirmatively: "Only what is known is that before he became what he was he called himself Cristobal Columbo de Terra-rubea and so did his brother Bartolome Colon".[17] In some Latin verses attributed to Bartolome, which probably were not his, this one was nevertheless signed as "Bartholomeus Columbus de Terra Rubea".[18] This mysterious "Terra Rubea" has been and still is one of the many puzzles from the life of the enigmatic Admiral. All efforts of Italian and Spanish researchers to find this elusive "Terra Rubea" from which the Columbus' brothers originated have been, so far, in vain. No satisfactory explanation for this problem has been offered.

But, the answer to this question may be found again if one

looks for it toward the Italian neighbors, the Croats, on the Northern shores of Adriatic.

Now, it happens that the entire South Dalmatia and other Southern regions were called since the earliest times "Red Croatia" (Croatia Rubea), Red Land or the country of the Red Croats. When the Croats settled in the 7th century in their new homeland along the Adriatic coast they called the Western part of their country "White Croatia" (Croatia Alba) and their Southern part "Red Croatia" (Croatia Rubea) according to their old Iranian (Sarmatian) customs and traditions by which the sides of the earth were marked by particular color—white was for West, red was for South. Various parts of the Adriatic coast of Croatia, Western and Southern, separatively, were also called Red Land or Cermnica (Terra Rubea). In Columbus' time, for example, a large part of the territory near Zadar was called "Cermnica" or Red Land (Terra Rubea). Zadar, incidentally, was the capital of Dalmatia in those times, sometime even the capital of all Croatia (Ladislaus V, of Naples was crowned in Zadar in 1403, and had its court there). Zadar was also the main naval port of Croatia and from 1358 was the seat of the Admiral of Croatia. The existence of Red Croatia and various Red Lands in Croatia was known in Venice in Columbus' time and was known even before Venice acquired Dalmatia in 1409, beginning with Andrea Dandolo (1309–1354), the Doge of Venice, and its principal chronicler. Christopher Columbus most likely was born in some part of ancient Red Croatia or South Croatia (probably in the region of Dubrovnik) which originally spread from the river of Cetina to Valona in today's Albania. Even the Albanians used to call the land North of Valona, "Kuchi" (Red Land). Also, the present name, Crna Gora (Montenegro) probably derives from Cermna Hora or Gora. (Red Croatia or Red Land), as the historian Milan Sufflay, the greatest expert on Illyrian (Albanian) history, points out.

Thus, we may assume that Christopher Columbus and his brother, by describing themselves as being from "Terra Rubea", meant some region in Croatia.[19]

This attribute, "de Terra Rubea", Columbus most probably adopted while residing in Venice and carried with him elsewhere and finally to Spain as Las Casas marked in his "Historia de las

Indias". It must be noted that such autodescription of Columbus "de Terra Rubea" while designating his original country as he knew it, at the same time remained as such only a vague description good enough to confound and throw off the track the individuals who may have been looking for the origin and the past of the enigmatic man, a past which Columbus for the reasons quite important for him wanted to remain secret. Taking into consideration the fact that Columbus knew Venice and resided in Venice there is really no other place Columbus could have pulled out this "Terra Rubea" and from the Venetian perspective it cannot mean anything other but some part of Dalmatia.[20]

5. Such a conclusion is supported by another peculiarity of Columbus: His apparent fondness for certain types of Greek letters. Of course, he was not Greek-born. Columbus, decidedly, was a man of Western culture and Western Catholic religion. This is beyond doubt, but several indications do point out that for the origin of Columbus we may have to look toward some Mediterranean country which was acquainted and influenced, at least a little, by Greek culture and Greek-orthodox religion. The original native land of Christopher Columbus seems to have been one Western-Catholic country which represented the borderland between the two cultures, Eastern and Western. Here, again, there is only one such Mediterranean country which fits the description: Croatia. The Croats settled, originally, the lands which once belonged to the Eastern, Byzantine Empire. Though they took their religion and culture from Rome, the Croats were thus unable to avoid being influenced a little, culturally and religiously by Byzantium Croatia was a borderland between the East and the West. Here, in Eastern Bosnia, the Drina River was a geographical as well as historical (since the division of Roman Empire made by Diocletian in 297) frontier between Eastern and Western Europe. Here the Romans divided the empire, here was the dividing line between the Eastern and the Western Church and between Eastern and Western culture.

One of the earliest influences of the Eastern culture the Croats experienced was the importation (by the Bulgarians) of the Greek-based Cyrillic alphabet which was, however, rearranged in Croatia into a separate Croatian version which was used up to the 20th century. This alphabet is usually called thee "Bosnian Alphabet" or "Croatian Cyrillic Alphabet" or, simply, the "Croatian letters". From the 12th century and throughout the Middle Ages this alphabet was very popular in Croatia and, particularly, in Columbus time. The Croatian-Bosnian alphabet was used also by the Turks themselves, not only in Bosnia, but in Istambul too. It was used by the tactful Venetians whenever they had to deal with their Croatian subjects in Dalmatia and, also, with Moslem and Catholic Croats in Bosnia. The Venetians, for example, kept a special paid scribe who translated and transcribed into the Croatian language and the Croatian Cyrillic alphabet all the official correspondence which was intended for those parts of Venetian Dalmatia which used those scriptures. Venice and Turkey even made official treaties in both the Croatian language and in this Greco-Croatian alphabet. In 1589, for example, Hodaverdi-chaush, the envoy of Turkish governor of Bosnia, Sofi Mehmed-pasha, made an agreement with the Venetian governor of Dalmatia, Francesco Zani, in which it is stated:

"So, we, Hodaverdi-chaush, willing to make this agreement, ordered that Alichehaya, who was with us in Zadar for this business, makes two copies in Turkish and two in Croatian" . . .[21]

In this Greco-Croatian alphabet we have to find the source for Columbus' inclination for letters using Greek forms. This seems to be the most logical explanation. Christoforo Colombo, the Genoese wool-weaver, certainly, never studied Greek. Columbus really never used any Greek letters. He only used two letters in his signature ("x" and "p") in such sense. ("x" as "H" and "p" as "r"). Those are also the letters from the Croatian cyrillic alphabet which was used exclusively by Croatian Catholics, Patharens and later Moslems (but never by the Greek-Orthodox.)

6. Significant and interesting also is the marginal note which Columbus made on the book "Historia rerum ubique gestarum" of Pope Pius II, in which he counted the years and the age of the world since Creation until 1481. He concluded that from the creation of the world to 1481, when he made the account, 5,241 years passed! This note strongly suggest that Columbus sometime used to count chronologically the years and the happenings from the creation and not from the time of Jesus Christ as was customary in the West. This was the Eastern, Byzantine way of

presenting the chronology of the world, which was, incidentally, very popular among Croatian Catholic clergy, particularly the Frenciscans (and Columbus, himself, was a lay member of the Franciscan order).

7. No less important is another statement of Columbus suggesting his Croatian origin in which he declared that he was acquainted and had discussions with scholars of Roman Catholic, Greek-Orthodox, Moslem and Jewish faiths as well as with those of many other sects! The question here is: Where did a Genoese wool-weaver who spent all his life in Genoa, Portugal, Spain and America acquaint himself with Greek-Orthodox religious scholars?

Here, again the most logical answer appears to be: Somewhere in Croatian lands. The Croats were the only Western Mediterranean people who actually possessed a population of the Greek Orthodox faith and had Greek Orthodox clergy. The Croats received their baptism from Rome and were originally all Roman Catholics. However, in the 12th century the Greek Orthodox religion was imported to some small parts of Croatia when the Byzantine emperor Emanuel I Comnenus conquered the Southern Croatian lands (Dalmatia, Bosnia and Hum or Herzegovina) and held them under his rule as "Kingdom of Croatia and Dalmatia" for thirteen years (1167–1180). Turkish invasions in the 14th and 15th century brought even more of Greek Orthodox into Croatian lands. In Columbus time the Greek Orthodox population in Croatia was already considerable.

Besides them, Croatia had in Columbus' time a large population of the Moslem religion. The Islamic faith was introduced first by the invading Turks in 1415. Furthermore, of particular importance is this part of Columbus' statement in which he mentioned that he had had discussions with those of many other sects (muchas otras sectas). This in Western, Catholic Europe can mean only the Patharens (Cathari). It just happened that in the 14th and 15th centuries probably 30% of all Croats followed the Patharenic heresy. Croatia also had a Jewish population, although not so numerous. Religious persecution of Jews was unknown in medieval Croatia. Numerous Jewish families from Spain found refuge in Croatia, mainly on the Dalmatian coast. It is not impossible that Columbus made his first contact and connaissance with Jews and Jewish learning exactly here (maybe in Dubrovnik and its surroundings). Still today in Dubrovnik there are some Jewish families whose ancestors came from Spain before Columbus was born. Some of them are still described by the place from which they hailed, such as Tolentino (Toledano) who came from Toledo in 1422. What is particularly important in this statement is that Columbus was well acquainted with people from all those religions, and Croatia was the only country in Europe which contained all those religious denominations. This points out that he was probably born somewhere in Croatia; otherwise his statement does not make much sense.[22]

8. Of particular interest are certain additional hints and statements of Columbus which suggest that the controversial Admiral was probably a native of the Kingdom of Croatia.

The first one concerns his notorious dream of a crusade and of the liberation of Jerusalem. The proponents of the theory that Columbus was a descendant of converted Jews have made a large story out of it, they say it is his Jewish origin speaking!

Now this is something rather puzzling, for the question is: Why Columbus wished and so ardently propagated the idea of a crusade and liberation of Jerusalem by the Christians if he was of Jewish extraction, and was allegedly conscious and proud of his Jewishness? And particularly when we take into account Columbus' own insistence on the old prophecy according to which "the one who will liberate Jerusalem will come from Spain". Why did Columbus want Jerusalem to be liberated by Spain, when in Spain, in his time, the Jewish people fared badly and, in fact, the same year Columbus took off from Palos all the Jews were expelled from Spain?

The idea of a crusade and the liberation of Jerusalem had nothing to do with the Jews in the Middle Ages as we all know well. The Croats, on the other hand, were very well acquainted with crusades and participated in them. In those times the "Templars" were the most popular order in Croatia; in fact, Croats and Hungarians themselves organized the 5th Crusade (1217–1218), which departed from Dalmatia and was led by Hungaro-Croatian king Andrew II, "The Jerusalemite", the former Regent of Croatia. The fever of crusades was always strong in Croatia and lasted thru centuries up to Columbus' time. And when the Crusades were already long forgotten the Croatian missionaries continued, individually, the work of the crusaders. It was not much before Columbus was born that a fellow Croat from Dalmatia, Nikola Tavelich, a native of Šibenik, died in 1391 as a martyr in Jerusalem (canonized in 1971).

It must also be noted that the Kings of Croatia, those from the Angevin dynasty of Naples (1301–1409) officially held the hereditary title of "King of Jerusalem" which is not entirely without significance. That title, the "King of Jerusalem", passed on to the Spanish (Aragonese) dynasty when it gained the Kingdom of Naples in 1443. With it also passed on to the Aragonese dynasty the pretensions and the rights to the thrones of Croatia and Hungary. Those rights were not recognized in Hungary, but were recognized to a considerable extent in Croatia. Alfonso V (1416–1458) the king of Aragon and Naples (and Jerusalem) whom Columbus most probably served in his youth not only held the royal title of Croatia but actually ruled in part of that country. And when the Turks conquered almost all of the Balkan peninsula in the 14th century, thus cutting the land route to Jerusalem, Croatia became the natural gathering point for most of the people of Central and Northwestern Europe making a pilgrimage to Holy Land. They would cross into Croatia from the North and usually gather in South Dalmatia, particularly in Dubrovnik, were they embarked on ships going to the Holy Land. In the 15th century, in Columbus' time, all year long South Croatia was full of people, mostly foreigners, commuting to Jerusalem. Some of them left notes of their passage thru Croatia. Columbus, by all indications, knew about all this traffic.

9. The same can be said for another notorious obsession of Columbus, that of a war against the Turks and Islam in general. Some say this comes from his Quixotic nature and they point out this was normal in Spain because of the long wars against the Moors during the Reconquista period. But this is a poor explanation: Columbus was not a Spaniard. Besides, he was totally engaged in his discoveries far away from the Islamic countries. Certainly his New World was not immediately menaced by the Turks, so why he worried so much? Here again it may be assumed that this anti-Turkish obsession of Columbus originated in Croatia. There the Turkish menace was real and the

Croats spent all that century and the next two trying to stop the Turks who began the conquest of Croatian lands in 1415 and, before Columbus died, occupied most of it. There was the real threat and the real frontier between Islam and Christian Europe. The Croats desperately defended themselves and in this way the entire Western Europe gave them the glorious but useless title of "Antemurale Christianitis" (The Frontal walls of Christianity) given to them in 1517, by the Genoese Pope Julius II.

10. It is noticeable, however, that Columbus was not so much hostile and rigidly anti-Jewish though he sometimes expressed a certain dislike and antipathy for both Jews and converted Jews. He acted more like a foreigner for whom the entire question was not emotionally, religiously and nationally so terribly important. This side of Columbus indicates again rather his Croatian origin than Genoese or Spanish taking in consideration how strong anti-Jewish was climate in those two countries.

In Croatian lands to the contrary, such a climate never existed and persecution was unknown. The good relations between Jews and Croats date from very early times and it is interesting to note that those relations originated exactly in Spain somewhere in 9th and 10th century, that is to say, in Moslem Spain, in the Caliphate of Cordoba where the Jews were so prominent. In fact this period of Spanish-Arab history is viewed by Jewish historians as the best and most glorious period of Arab-Jewish cooperation and a great page in the history of the Jewish people. In Arab Spain the Croats also played a great role. From the 9th to the 12th century, the Caliphate employed Croats as soldiers who constituted the personal guard of the Caliph. The guard initially was composed of Croats who were taken prisoner by Arabs and also by Venetians, who subsequently sold them to Arabs, but later the Croats came freely into the service of the Caliphate as soldiers of fortune. The Croatian guard numbered up to 6,000 men and often held the pivotal position in Arab Spain. The Croats were given many important posts including the dignity of "Hadjib" (Prime minister). For example, during the period of 1009–1013, the Hadjib Wadha El Ameri, a Croatian, was the virtual and absolute ruler of Arab Spain who gave all positions in his Caliphate to his Croats.[23]

In his study "Jews and Croats in Arab Spain", Jewish historian

Lavoslav Glesinger noted the fact that in Arab Spain, the cultural participation of the Arabs themselves was small. The cultural and often the political life of the Caliphate was created in most of the cases by foreigners. In this culture, nominally Arab, one of the principal roles. Glesinger says, was played by Jews and Croats, among whom mutual friendship and cooperation existed. In this period the relations between the Kingdom of Croatia and the Caliphate of Cordoba were very lively and, he says, the political, cultural and economic interchange was particularly devoloped by Croatian king Tomislav and in those relations the Jews played an important role. The kings of Croatia regularly employed Jews as their counselors and diplomats. In 953, Glesinger says, an embassy of Croatian king Kresimir II, arrived in Cordoba, among whom two of the envoys were Mar Saul and Mar Josef; i. e., both ambassadors of Croatia were Jews.[24]

Later, as has already been noted, a number of Jewish families from Spain found refuge (in the 14th and 15th century) in Croatia, particularly in the region of South Dalmatia, where some of their descendants still can be found today. The Jews who settled in South Croatia enjoyed complete freedom and in the otherwise strictly Catholic Dubrovnik, the Jewish faith was the only other officially recognized and permitted religion.

This helps to explain Columbus' attitude toward Jews and also the fact that he knew very well the Old Testament and some other Jewish writings. The knowledge of the Old Testament and Jewish history was however, nothing extraordinary for a Croatian of Columbus' time; it was normal. The habit of looking into the ancient history of Israel and writing about Biblical themes from the Old Testament was a recognized trend in Croatian literature. It is enough to mention, for example, the contemporary epic "Judita" written by the Dalmatian nobleman Marko Marulić. It is one of the greatest works in Croatian literature and in fact in European as well. It was written in 1501, and later published in Venice (of course) in 1521, under the title: "The book of Marko Marulo from Split which contains the history of the saint widow Judith, in Croatian verses composed, how she killed the Duke Holofernes in the midst of his army and liberated the people of Israel of great peril."

According to its title and content one would believe this to be a Jewish work, but it is not. Marulić took the then common theme from the Old Testament and his purpose was to encour- , age his fellow Croats who were then fighting desperately for their survival facing the never ending invasions of the Turks, to take an example from the history and experience of Israel and to continue in their resistance to Turkish invaders, as did the ancient Israeli fighters for freedom against foreign agressors.

In light of this all Columbus' good knowledge of Old Testament and some of his references to Jews. Jewish history or Jewish leanings becomes much more understandable. For a Spaniard or a Genoese (even if he was of remote Jewish origin) it looked somewhat odd, but for a contemporary Croatian it was nothing particularly strange. The apparent innocence and unwariness which he exhibited sometime while referring to the Jews only reinforces the likelihood that he was a total stranger who did not fully understand the religious situation in Spain in regard to the Jews and did not fully grasp the seriousness and danger which some of his remarks may have contained. A Catholic and such an intelligent one born in a rigorous Catholic country, be it Genoa or Spain, knew perfectly well how perilous it was to exhibit anything which would not sit well with the opinion of the Holy Office. Certain opinions of Columbus which were not exactly in accord with those of the Inquisition can hardly be ascribed to a Genoese born of Spanish-Jewish ancestry, but only to a foreigner, in this case a Croatian, who did not entirely comprehend that what he was saying may have had serious consequences for him.

11. Christopher Columbus' Croatian extraction is also inferred by his equally problematic name which is no less complex and had been also one of many mysteries which gave no small headache to researchers. During a period of about seventeen years Columbus changed his name five times! The historians are amazed by those acrobatics in his family name. Their question is: Why?

As many point out,including Salvador de Madariaga, there is nothing unusual in the name Colombo—the form of this name is perfectly good in Spanish, too, there are numerous Spanish names similar to it, and even the name Colombo appears in

Spain somewhat later, so, why did Columbus and his brothers changed it so often?

Salvador de Madariaga theorizes that Columbus' family was a Jewish-Catalan family named Colom which migrated to Italy in the previous century and changed its name to Columbo and that Christopher Columbus, now in the service of Spain, merely reverted to his old family name.[25]

To this it must be said the following: There is not a single proof, a single indication, that any of the Colombo families (for there were, apparently, several Colombo families in Genoa) was of Jewish origin, neither that one ever came from Spain, neither that one was ever called Colom. Furthermore, Columbus' final and official name was Colon not Colom. This is the name which all his descendants bear. Salvador de Madariaga thinks Columbus further refashioned his name because of the advantages of the Castilian form Colon over the Catalan Colom and from the psychological impact of the word "colonizing".[26] In other words Columbus discovered new lands across the Ocean and saw himself as a colonizer of the New World. Thus, Colon equals colonizer!

But, this cannot be accepted. Columbus used the name Colon many years before he discovered the new lands and before he came to Spain in 1485. He used it previously in Portugal too. The King of Portugal John II, in a letter to Columbus in 1488, four years before the discovery, calls him Colon (Collon). Therefore, the name Colon or some form very close to it must have been the original name of Christopher Columbus. Fernando Colon, his son and biographer, believes that there is certain mystery in those variations of his father's name while Bartolome de Las Casas says that Colon was probably his original name. Even Peter Martyr who gives Columbus vaguely as a Ligurian in his Latin "Decades" never calls him Columbus (Colombo) but always Colonus (Colon). Thus here we have Bartolome de Las Casas who may have known Columbus and had his personal papers at his disposal and who, even if he did not know the Admiral himself, in any case personally knew his two brothers, the Adelantado Don Bartolome and the younger Diego. And here we have, also, Fernando Colon, the son of the Discoverer, who, of course, knew his own father and his own two uncles, but both of them do not know where Columbus was born, they do not know even, for sure, what his original name was!

Whoever studies the problem calmly, without a pre-conceived notion and without passion, I believe, will agree that it is pretty unlikely that Columbus and his brothers were Genoese-born, for if they were plain Colombos from Genoa, their exact Genoese origin would have been too obvious to be concealed from those two men who were so close to them (and we must always re-member that Fernando Colon personally visited Genoa and its surroundings in a vain search for his father's family—of which he found no trace). Therefore, we must agree with Fernando Colon's assertion that there is some mystery in his father's name. The mystery obviously points out that he did not come originally from a place so well known as Genoa, but from some much more distant country. To tackle the problem of Columbus' name it is necessary again to go back to Adriatic and Dalmatia. In the first place it must be noted, as it was already said, that Columbus' frequent change and refashioning of the name is unusual for an Italian. On the contrary, for a Croatian, particularly an Adriatic Croat this was a habit, a tradition. Because the Croats usually had their names in Slavic forms, those names were generally incomprehensible and hard for foreigners to write correctly, thus, throughout the centuries it was a frequent habit for Croats to change or refashion their names to fit the particular environ-ment in which they lived in foreign countries. And even in their own country the Croats tended to Italianize their names and did so in great number, not only in the Venetian occupied Istra and Dalmatia but also in what remained Free Croatia (Southern Dal-matia with Dubrovnik).

When this is known it is much easier to understand why Columbus had a habit of changing and refashioning his family name. The first name Columbus used when he arrived in Por-tugal was apparently Columbo. We may assume that Columbus originally had a name similar to this one which was refashioned in Venice into Columbo and that he carried this name with him thru Italy, Spain and Portugal until about 1476. But, it is also possible, and I believe much more likely, that he temporarily adopted this name only when he arrived in Lisbon.

When Columbus reached Portugal he was a total stranger

there. But, being a Dalmatian Croat, who spent a considerable time in Italy and spoke good enough Italian, it was natural that he gravitated toward the Italian colony there; and in Lisbon there was one large colony of Genoese. Under the circumstances those Genoese-Italians were for him and his brother Bartolome the closest thing to their own kind; in short, they were practically like compatriots to them.[27] It is also very possible that he re-fashioned his name into Columbo according to the name of that famous French Admiral-pirate Guillome de Casanave Coullon with whom Columbus sailed as a pirate for several years and who, importantly, was called Colombo in Italy and Colon in Spain. But, since Columbo was not his real name,he dropped it soon never to use it again.

It is interesting to note that Columbus apparently called him-self Columbo not Colombo like those in Genoa. Columbo is the Croatian form for Columbus and this also represents an indi-cation of his Croatian origin. The habit of pronouncing the letter "o" like "u" is a very well-known characteristic of Adriatic Croats.[28] In Venice they also pronounce it that way, further suggesting that Columbus belongs to the Adriatic. In his tran-script of the alleged letter of Toscanelli which he allegedly re-ceived in Portugal in 1474, Columbus, himself, writes his name as Columbo (with "u"). Also so does Las Casas.

As for the name Columbo (Colombo) and any other name Columbus used or was reported to have used there is no problem in finding similar or equivalent names among the Croats. For example, among the Croats there are such names as Kolumbić (Kolumbich), Columbini, Colombini, Columbani, Columbarich. Every one of them in other Italian form comes out as Columbo (Colombo). And as it can be seen, some such Croatian names like, Columbini, Colombini, Columbani, coming from Venetian Dalmatia are already in Italian form. Also Croatian names Golub, Golubić, Golubović in Italianized form mean Columbo. But, Columbus' real name was, obviously, Colon. Many efforts were made to trace this name and to explain it. In Spain, of course, it exists and is frequent, but, since most of historians are stuck with the notion that Columbus came from Italy, the problem arises: No such name in Italy! But, the equivalent for Columbus' official name exists in Croatia. This is the well known Croatian name Kolonić (Colonich). That Croatian name Kolonić and the Spanish name Colon are two forms of the same name. Christopher Columbus, who probably bore such a name in his native Dalmatia must have noticed the remarkable similarity of the Spanish name, Colon, with his own and this was most likely the reason why he adopted this name as the official one for him and for all his successors. In his testament he ordered that all his descendants must call themselves "de Colon" and this is the exact duplicate of Croatian name Kolonić (Colonich) given in Spanish form. The "-ić" (-ich) in this name and in all other Croatian names is a suffix, it has the same meaning as "de" in Spanish ("of" in English). Thus Colonich means exactly "de Colon"! Bartolome de Las Casas seems to have been right when he said that Colon was most probably his original name.[29]

The name Kolonić is very frequent in Croatia, it can be found virtually in any part of the country, and, what is of further significance, numerous Kolonić families were noble, which is in total accordance with Columbus' claim that he was a descendant of a noble family which once was prominent. This noble Croatian origin is also further indicated by the fact that Columbus had his original coat-of-arms: A blue bend on a gold field with a red chief.

That Columbus' coat-of-arms has been always under severe attacks by numerous "Columbus was a Genoese" believers for the obvious reason: A noble Columbus is incompatible with the Genoese plebeian Christoforo Colombo. Some writers say that in those times even the middle class people and members of trade guilds often had coats-of-arms, so, this would have been, they suggest, his father's wool-weaver's coat-of-arms! Others believed that he simply invented this blazon to make himself look like nobleman. They point out that all noble families called Colombo in Italy, Colom in Aragon and Colon in Castile, regularly have a common feature in their arms, a dove.[30] Thus, if Columbus was originally a nobleman he would have had a dove featured in his blazon. This, of course, is true if a person was Italian or Spanish-born, but Columbus was not, and the absence of a dove further suggests, indirectly, his Croatian origin, for if he was an Italian or a Spaniard he would have known perfectly well that the dove is a common feature in all arms of the noble families Colombo in Italy and Colom and Colon in Spain and he would have, undoubtedly, inserted a dove in his allegedly original coat-of-arms to make it look true and authentic. The fact that he never did this only proves that this blazon was really his original and that, in reality, he had nothing to do with Colombos in Italy and Coloms and Colons in Spain. This is in perfect accord with Croatian hypothesis and fits fine the facts: The name Kolonić (Colonich) in the Croatian language has no connection whatsoever with the word "dove".[31]

12. It should also be added that the first names of Columbus and his brothers were typical and commonly used Croatian names: The names Christopher (Krsto), Bartolome (Bartol) and Diego or Giacomo (Jakov), were just about the most frequent names among Adriatic Croats in Columbus time. It is interesting, furthermore, to note that the names of Christopher and Bartholomeus were particularly frequent in the Frankopan (Frankapan) family. This leading Croatian family owned as their private property several entire provinces of the Kingdom of Croatia. This family had six Bans (Viceroys) of Croatia and in Columbus time was her premier family. From the 15th to the 17th century the name Christopher occurs in almost every generation of this family![32]

Columbus' somewhat younger contemporary was Christopher Frankopan (1482–1527), the Ban of Croatia and a Croatian national hero ("Protector regni") who was famous in all Europe. He served, initially, the Emperor Maximilian I, and was the Generallissimus of the army of The Holy Roman Empire in the war against Venice from which he took the entire Furlandy, but was taken prisoner. Since France wanted his services he was delivered in 1519 to the French king Francis I. In 1523, he returned home from France and in 1525, with a band of volunteers, led the famous march to relieve Jajce, the only Croatian stronghold which was left in Turkish occupied Bosnia. He was also the principal supporter of the Spanish prince Ferdinand, then the Archduke of Austria in his pretentions to the throne of Croatia. The Archduke of Austria was, of course, the grandson of Catholic kings Ferdinand and Isabella and brother of Spanish king and Holy Roman emperor Charles V, (The Hapsburgs gained the Spanish throne like everything else—thru marriage).

Christopher Frankopan, himself, thought that with the Archduke on the throne and Charles V and Spain behind him, the Croats would not only be able to save that what was left of Croatia, after Turkish conquests, but, eventually, to regain the lost territories. In fact with Ferdinand's help he was preparing the ground for the liberation of Bosnia. Here it is interesting to note that this Christopher Frankopan was himself half-Spaniard and related to the old royal house of Spain. His mother was the Spanish princess Luisa of Aragon.

Whether this all had any bearing on Christopher Columbus finding his way to Spain to the service of the House of Aragon is unknown, but it is, in any case, a vivid illustration of the close ties the Croatian people had with Spain in Columbus' time. Those ties, undoubtedly, made it possible for Columbus to find his way to the Iberian peninsula and to his destiny—nothing unusual for a Croatian of his time.[33]

13. Although it is difficult to prove this because Columbus used only Spanish as his habitual and official language, there are actually good indications that he knew some other non-Latin language and that he even used a different alphabet and thus it is even possible, indirectly, to conclude that this language was most probably Croatian.

As was mentioned before, Columbus had little mastery of Italian. He knew it well enough but it was not his mothers tongue, it was a learned one and an imperfectly learned one at that. Neither was Spanish his original language and of course, neither was Latin, from which it logically follows that the language in which he was born was certainly some different one, non-Latin. If one follows Bartolome de Las Casas, Columbus' admirer and defender, who had the Columbus diary as well as many other personal papers, one has to reach such a conclusion. In his "History of the Indies" Las Casas expressed several significant comments in regard to the language of the Admiral. For example: "Those were his words, not much polished in our romance, but he certainly should not be deprecated for this" . . . "Those were his words though defective in our Castilian language which he did not know well" . . . "Those are his formal words, although some of them not in perfect Castilian romance, because it was not the maternal language of Admiral" . . . "All those are the words of Admiral with his humble lack of proper vocabulary and style, because he was not a native of Castile" . . .

Las Casas notes several times that Columbus shows in his manner of speech to be "a native speaker of some other language because he cannot penetrate and grasp completely the vocabulary of the Castilian language, nor its way of speaking.[34]

The careful examination of those notations of Las Casas shows that Columbus did not speak Spanish well either. The vocabulary as well as the construction and spirit of the Spanish language is strange to him. But this fact also in a way excludes Italian as the original language of the Discoverer. We must note that Italian and Spanish are closely related languages, both drown from Latin with similar vocabulary (a Spaniard and an Italian can understand each other quite well). The construction of the Italian language, spirit and expression is basically the same as in Spanish. Why were that spirit and expression, so common in those two Latin languages, difficult for Columbus to grasp? His original language, obviously was a non-Latin one and responsible for his difficulty in penetrating the significance and the spirit of Latin-based Spanish language.

With respect to the original language of Columbus even, more important is the declaration made in 1515 by Garcia Ferrando, the physician of Palos, who described Columbus in occasion of his arrival at the Monastery of La Rabida in 1491, and said of the impression he made on Fray Juan Perez de Marchena:

"He (Columbus) looked like a man from another country or kingdom and stranger in his language".[35]

This means that Columbus, after five years in Spain (and probably many years before,) still gave the impression of a complete stranger, not an Italian, Genoese, related to and so familiar to Spaniards. The very same expression used to describe Columbus (from another country or kingdom and stranger in his language"!) practically excludes Genoa as possible fatherland of Admiral. He looked and sounded as a total stranger from some distant kingdom . . .

14. The humanist Peter Martyr d'Anghiera in his "Decades" supplies another very important detail which permit us to conclude that this faraway land from which Columbus hailed was, indeed, the Kingdom of Croatia. He wrote that when Com-

mander Francisco de Bobadilla was sent to Hispaniola, in 1500, as a special royal commissary and new governor, to investigate the disastrous state of affairs and misgovernment of Columbus and his brothers, those three were for a moment disposed to resist him, even by armed forces, though the royal credentials of Bobadilla superposed those of Columbus and gave him full delegation of royal authority to establish the order.

Columbus—wrote Peter Martyr—sent his brother the Adelantado Bartolome who was away in the other part of the island, some letters written in "unknown characters" in which they said he informed his brother of the situation caused by the arrival of Bobadilla and instructed him to come to his aid with armed men in case the new governor tried to use force to remove him from his office of Viceroy and Governor-General.[36] Those letters written in "unknown characters" fell in the hands of Bobadilla who sent them to the King and Queen of Spain. This curious detail about which, as Salvador de Madariaga says, nobody raised question is extremely important. In light of what was already said here about Columbus, this detail is nothing short of sensational, for it constitutes another proof of Columbus' Croatian origin.

What were these "unknown characters", what kind of alphabet was used there? Well, Columbus was undoubtedly, ethnically and geographically a Mediterranean man of Western culture and Western Catholic religion—nobody will dispute that. The Croats too, were a Mediterranean people of Western culture and Western Catholic religion, but they were the only such people which beside the Latin alphabet also had their own two traditional national alphabets. The one such, as was already mentioned, was called Bosnian or Croatian Cyrillic alphabet which was based on Greek.[37] But this one was not used by Columbus for those letters then would not have been mentioned as of "unknown characters", anybody with little education or any priest would have easily identified those characters as a kind of Greek alphabet.

Thus the other, the oldest and original Croatian alphabet was used, the one which is commonly called the Glagolitic alphabet.

The origins of this alphabet were brought by Croats (Alans) and Goths to the ancient Roman land of Dalmatia between the

4th and the 7th century when the Alano-Gothic state of Croatia was founded along the Northern shores of the Adriatic. That alphabet, obviously defective, was polished and given final touches in ancient Roman Dalmatia and was widely used in all Croatian lands through centuries and particularly in Columbus' time. According to traditions of the Croatian Catholic clergy in Dalmatia, particularly the Franciscans, this alphabet was invented by St. Hyeronimus the patron saint of Dalmatia (died in 420) who, is said, created this alphabet for the use of Alano-Gothic (Croatian) conquerors. The alphabet was also known throughout the Middle Ages as St. Hyeronimus' alphabet. (Incidentally, as it can be seen from his writings Columbus was familiar with this Dalmatian saint and patron St. Hyeronimus, which is quite natural for a Dalmatian).[38] It is more probable that St. Hyeronimus and other Roman clergy did not invent this alphabet, they only perfected it. The Latin clergy in Croatia, as can be seen from the oldest sources always mention this alphabet as "Gothic letters" for the original Latin inhabitants of Dalmatia called all the Croats "Goths". This means that, basically, this alphabet was brought by the Croats into Dalmatia. Still in 12th century the anonymous Latin priest from Dioclea (Bar) who translated to Latin the chronicle "Kingdom of the Croats" which was written in the Croatian language and in Glagolitic letters circa 1078, called it "Libellus Gothorum" (The Booklet about the Goths).

The Glagolitic alphabet shows certain similarity with various alphabets from Biblical lands of the Middle East and it was this glagolitic alphabet Columbus undoubtedly used in his secret correspondence with his brother. Pending a proof to the contrary this must be accepted as a fact, for there is no other viable explanation about Columbus writing in "letters of unknown characters", there is no other alternative to it and for Westerners and all non-Croatians those letters and their shape were truly both unknown and baffling.

This also helps to explain another curious detail about Columbus—his nickname "King Pharaoh" which was given to him by Spaniards on Hispaniola. When Columbus was stripped of his powers and taken in chains to Spain the accusations and complaints of the Spanish colonists flowed like a river against the

Admiral and his brothers. One of the most intriguing comments was the of Father Juan de Trasierra who wrote to Cardinal Cisneros who was in charge of the affairs of the Indies begging him to free this land (Hispaniola) from the domination of "King Pharaoh" and make sure that neither Columbus nor any of "his nation" ever returns to the islands of New World.

The vague and unspecified expression "any of his nation" indicates that the settlers on Hispaniola were not really sure who the Columbus brothers were and from where they came. The unidentified "his nation" for all intents and purposes excludes Genoa, and such an expression could not have been used to describe the Conversos either.

The origin of Columbus nickname "King Pharaoh" obviously sprang from his obscure Croatian origin (unknown to the settlers of Hispaniola) and from the discovery of those "unknown" Glagolitic letters Columbus used in his secret correspondence with his brother which was intercepted and sent back to Spain.

The Croatian glagolitic alphabet is an unique alphabet which shows some similarities and possible links with several ancient alphabets of the Middle East. Many of researchers have studied those links. A number of them believe the Croatian glagolitic alphabet originated there. This suggest that the discovery of Columbus' secret correspondence created the impression on Hispaniola that the three brothers Columbus, those three mysterious foreigners who kept to themselves must have come from those regions of the Eastern Mediterranean. Thus Columbus' nickname of "King Pharaoh" was created, of course, with this name Spanish colonists meant also a despot.

The precious detail about Columbus' nickname supplied by Father Juan de Trasierra compliments the one furnished by Peter Martyr about the Admiral's secret correspondence in letters of "unknown characters" practically showing that behind the name of "Colon-King Pharaoh" stood in reality one Croatian adventurer.

To arrive at such a conclusion one has to mention, for example, the famous Croatian quaresmal Glagolitic manuscript which is preserved today in the Municipal Library of Oporto in Portugal

This manuscript originated in Croatia in Columbus time, circa 1460, the one in Oporto is a copy made probably around 1480.

The manuscript contains the religious sermons, but in the 16th century some historical notes have been added to it about the attacks of the Turks, the fall of the city of Novigrad and the death of the Croatian captain Tudor. In the 18th century this manuscript somehow found its way to Portugal and eventually ended up in the Library of Oporto when it opened to the public in 1833. This Croatian Glagolitic manuscript baffled Portuguese scholars as well as some foreign ones. The "mysterious" document was compared with letters of Ethiopian or Amharic, Pali, Burmese, Javanese, Indo-Hyamarite etc., with some of the scholars declaring the manuscript to be written in an unknown language and characters, others proposed that it must be Chaldean, Himyarite or Ethiopian. The majority settled for Ethiopian.[39] It was not until 1880 that the document was definitively identified. During the International Congress of Anthropology in Lisbon, Adolf Pawinski the professor of Warsaw University and Portuguese slavist Dom Aniceto dos Reis Goncalves Vianna visited the Library of Oporto and examined its mysterious document. They recognized immediately in it a Croatian Glagolitic manuscript.[40]

It is interesting that the first librarian of the Municipal Library of Oporto, Dom Diogo do Goes Lara de Andrade after careful examination and comparison with other alphabets in 1833, originally catalogued the manuscript under the number 639, correctly as "codice sclavonico em caracteres dos denominados Illyricos ou de S. Jeronimo" (Codex Slavonian in characters called Illyrians or of St. Hyeronimus). But other scholars who followed just could not believe that such an alphabet could be European, particularly from a people like the Croats, Western and Catholic.[41]

Now, if modern 19th century linguistic experts could have been confounded by Croatian Glagolitic letters and took it for Middle Eastern or Ethiopian those letters must have looked even more like such in 1500 to the generally simple crowd of Spanish colonists on Hispaniola. This precious detail furnished by Peter Martyr about the Admiral's secret correspondence written in "letters of unknown characters" is one of the strongest proofs that Christopher Columbus was in reality a Croatian. It will be difficult for anybody to throw any evidence against such a conclusion. To do so he will have to find some other alternative for Columbus' secret correspondence and nobody has found one, so far, for the task is seemingly impossible; No Italian, a remote Italo-Spanish Converso, Spaniard, Portuguese or Frenchman could have ever used an unknown and mysterious alphabet.

Only a Croatian of his time could have written in "letters of unknown characters" . . .

Those letters which Columbus wrote to his brother were intercepted, as Peter Martyr says, and sent to Spain to the King and Queen. Where those mysterious letters ended-up and what the King Ferdinand and Queen Isabella did with them nobody knows. If this correspondence only could be found somewhere, the question of the nationality of Christopher Columbus would be resolved.

It is interesting and important to note here that the best example of Croatian Glagolitic scriptures, contemporary to Columbus, is the "Colonich Collection" ("Kolonićev Zbornik") from the year 1486. As it can be seen its author has the same name as Columbus in Spanish: Colonich in Spanish form means "de Colon"!

15. Another interesting indication of the Croatian origin of Columbus is found written in his Journal as Las Casas renders it and it is inserted into the pages of his log, dated Thursday 14th of February 1493, during his return from the first voyage of discovery, when Columbus and his crew were heading home thru a violent storm which made them believe to be lost and when everyone feared never to make it home to Spain:

" . . . The Admiral issued an order that a pilgrimage should be made to Our Lady of Guadalupe with a candle of 5 pound of weight in wax, and that the entire crew must take the oath and that the pilgrimage was to be made by 'the one on whom the lot fell . . . Then another lot was drawn to send someone to pilgrimage to Santa Maria of Loreto, which is in the march of Ancona, in papal territory, a place where Our Lady made and makes today many great miracles. The lot was drawn by a sailor named Pedro de Villa to whom the Admiral promised to pay for his expenses . . . "

Now, this is very interesting. Here we have a crew of Spaniards and only one foreigner—the Admiral himself. And the order for a pilgrimage to Our Lady of Loreto came from Columbus himself. But, how did it happen that a Genoese turned Spaniard, or possibly a Spaniard, on the middle of Atlantic picks a shrine in the Adriatic zone to make a pilgrimage?

It must be noted here that it was a tradition and practically a must for medieval Croats to make a pilgrimage to Italy, their neighboring country. Every year since immemorial times thousands and thousands of Croatian pilgrims headed for Italy to visit the Holy shrines. The faith of those Croatian pilgrims did not escape Dante Alighieri, who, nearly two centuries earlier in his "La Divina Comedia" noted in his verses (Paradise xxxi):

"Qual'e colui che Forse di Croazia

Viene a veder la Veronica nostra" . . .

(Like a man who maybe from Croatia comes to see our Veronica).

And the medieval Croats (same as the modern), were always very devout worshipers of Mary ("The Queen of the Croats"). It just happens that Ancona and Our Lady of Loreto were traditional and the most popular destinations to which almost all Croatian pilgrims invariably came. Every Croatian Christian knew Santa Maria de Loreto like Columbus knew and remembered the shrine the middle of the Atlantic. Loreto was for all purpose a Croatian shrine. The spiritual importance of Our Lady of Loreto for Croatian people is shown by the fact that the first college for the education of Croatian clergy, the "Collegium illyricum Lauretanum" was founded exactly in Loreto in 16th century.

More importantly, this college was founded by Pope Gregory XIII (1572–1585) specifically for the education of Croatian national Glagolitic clergy, that is for those clergy who since the 7th century used—by special permission given by Rome—in Catholic services and in Mass the Croatian language instead of the Latin and used in scriptures exclusively the Croatian national Glagolitic alphabet, the one which Columbus undoubtedly also knew and used in his private correspondence with his brother as was previously mentioned.[42]

The fact that Columbus selected the shrine in the Adriatic zone whose main distinction was that it was the favorite shrine of the Croatian people indicates strongly that Christopher Columbus had some connection with that people.

16. Speaking of religion for the purpose of determining the true national origin of Christopher Columbus and to prove convincingly that he was of Croatian extraction, the subject must be also looked further into from the religious point of view. Although Columbus was a Christian, a Roman Catholic, through careful study one can perceive a certain vagueness in his religious consciousness, some uncertainty when it came to ecclesiastic matters. A devout Catholic, he, however, showed some weaknesses and faulty knowledge of some Catholic dogmas; sometimes he expressed some opinions which were not always in complete accordance with contemporary teachings of the Catholic Church and the doctrine of the Holy Office or Inquisition.

Those statements of Columbus made innocently and completely unaware of their true meaning have some scholars confused. Some of them proposed that Columbus may have been a Converso, that is, a descendant of Jews who converted to the Catholic religion. Salvador de Madariaga, the champion of this school, based the main part of his argument on this supposed indication trying to prove from any possible (and impossible) angle that Christoforo Colombo of Genoa descended from a family of converted Spanish (Catalan) Jews.

As it was already noted, particularly by Madariaga, Bartolome de Las Casas has made some rather strange remarks about the religion of the official Discoverer. He seemed insecure on this point and somewhat wondering: "In what concerns the Christian religion he was, without doubt, a Catholic and of much devotion," said Las Casas, and then noted furthermore: "All said of origin and Fatherland and lineage and parents . . . and also of Christianity what was known in Christopher Columbus . . . " And this particularly: "Seeing himself very weak as Christian, and certainly he was, he received all the sacraments with much devotion.[43]

The question is now: Why those strange remarks of Las Casas concerning the religion of Columbus? Why if he was Genoese, talking about "of what was known of Christianity" in him (like something is missing or unknown), why he was "without doubt" a devout Catholic and why he was again "certainly a weak Christian"?

Those are the remarks of Las Casas which Salvador de Madariaga cites too and those are the questions he also poses and immediately answers by declaring that it all becomes clear if we accept the hypothesis that Columbus was of Jewish ancestry.[44] Madariaga also mentions the statement Columbus made in his Journal under the date of November 27, 1492, and given textually by Las Casas. This is the passage: "And I say that Your Highnesses must not permit that any foreigner, except Catholic Christians, trade or set foot here, because this was the beginning and purpose of this enterprise made for the increase and the glory of the Christian religion; no one should come here who is not a Good Christian".[45]

Madariaga, surprisingly, interprets those words as being almost an admission of Columbus being a Converso. He thinks that with the phrase "Good Christians" Columbus meant the Conversos for whom the door of the New World should remain open! He says this is a symptom exclusively of Jewishness because Columbus does not speak only of "old Christians" (original Christians), but also of "good Christians" and those are the Conversos! This, says Madariaga, constitutes one further indication that Columbus was of Converso descent.[46]

How the renowned scholar arrived at this wholly fantastic deduction I do not know. The argument rests on absolutely nothing. It was simply invented to explain what is unexplainable in the traditionally established notion of Christoforo Colombo, Genoese, because it does not fit that notion. There is nothing to suggest that with the phrase "Good Christians" Columbus was referring to Conversos with whom he allegedly sympathized. The Conversos in Spain were never called "Good Christians", but "New Christians" (Los Nuevos Cristianos) as opposed to old Christians. There is nothing in this statement to indicate that he was a Jew.

However, it is true that Columbus showed certain weaknesses in his understanding of some Catholic dogma and it seems true that the term "Good Christians" had certain meaning for him. What he meant by this expression nobody knew, so far, for sure. But, with the Croatian hypothesis this question is easily resolved, all vacilations and weaknesses explained and Columbus decidedly shown to have been in reality of Croatian extraction. There was nothing elusive, mysterious or remotely Jewish about those "Good Christians". Simply, in the 13th, 14th and 15th centuries—in Columbus' time—the ancient territory of the Kingdom of the Croats was full of Good Christians. That's right, of Good Christians!

In the 10th century a certain Bulgarian priest named Jeremy, the self-called Bogumil ("Dear to God"), constructed from the old dualistic Manichean religion and some contemporary Christian beliefs a new religion commonly called the Bogumilian religion. The new faith spread through the Balkans and was imported by Bulgarians into certain regions of Croatia; in the first place to the mountainous region of Bosnia where the Roman Catholic faith, due to geographical conditions was somewhat fluid. The Croats there, being themselves originally mostly Iranians (Alans) and retaining many of the original Manichean beliefs, (for Manicheanism was a mixture of Christian beliefs and the old Iranian religion of Zarathustra), accepted this new faith.[47] From Bosnia this heresy spread farther and from the 13th to the 15th century possibly a third of the Croatian population followed this faith. The fight against this heresy among the Croats was one of the main preoccupation of Rome and of the Catholic Churches of Western Europe, the Spanish in particular.

The religious doctrine of the followers of this sect was essentially the same as that of the Patharens (Cathari) of the West, though there were among them various currents, and sometime their sect would come close to many Catholic beliefs and customs. The Bosnian heretics are usually called the Bogumils (from their founder) and on the Balkan peninsula and that name is accepted today by local historiography; in Rome and in Western Europe they were always called Patharens and Manicheans. They themselves, however, never used any such description. They always called themselves "Good Christians" and only sometimes, "True Christians".[48] Their exact religious philosophy and their relation to the Roman Catholic church is still a matter of discussion. There are opinions that Croatian Good Christians were not in reality Manichean heretics but just "undeveloped Catholics". It is pointed out that they did not call themselves at all Patharens, nor used any other names known for heretics, they simply called themselves "Good Christians".[49] That's why, in the beginning, they obtained the official approval and the benediction of Rome.

There is some truth in this contention, but there cannot be doubt of their essentially Patharenic nature. They were similar to the Patharens (Cathari) of Western Europe with whom they maintained regular ties; in fact, Italian Patharens traveled to Bosnia to learn about the true Patharenism.[50]

By the middle of the 14th century Bosnia and Hum (Herzegovina) were almost entirely Patharenic (Good Christian) and this sect spread also to other regions, particularly to South Dalmatia. Most of the nobility in those regions belonged to the Good Christians. This heresy was eradicated only in the second part of 15th century with the vigorous work of local clergy, almost exclusively Franciscans, Rome, and numerous missionaries from Western Europe and, in the final analysis, by the Turks who in the end conquered Bosnia. (The last Good Christian in Croatian lands disappeared around 1520).

It can be assumed with considerable certainty that Christopher Columbus descended from one such noble Good Christian family which reverted to Catholicism. Of course, his use of the phrase "Good Christians" was done in complete unwariness and innocence; it was probably a habit he derived from his native country. This phrase which had, in fact, a double meaning and was also applicable to any good Catholic, was not dangerous for him because the Croatian heretics were known in Spain and Western Europe always as "Patharens" and "Manicheans".

That Christopher Columbus was very familiar with "Good Christians" and that he probably descended from those Croatian heretics can be easily deduced from his already mentioned statement:

"I had discussions and conversations with scholars both, ecclesiastic and secular, Latin and Greek, Jewish and Moorish and with many from the other sects."[51]

Note the phrase: "and with many from the other sects" . . . This in Western, Catholic Mediterranean can mean only the Patharens! This would, thus, explain his vacilations and incomplete knowledge of contemporary doctrine of Catholic church and his use of the word "Good Christians". It as already said that the family of the Admiral comes most probably from Dalmatia. Well, in the 14th and 15th centuries South Dalmatia was full of Patharens. Roman Catholic clergy in those parts of Croatia were incessantly occupied in the conversion of those so-called Good Christians. In 1403, the envoys from Dubrovnik briefed King Sigismund of the great expenses they were incurring in converting the Patharens "from Bosnian religion to Christianity", and building churches for the new converts.[52] In 1431, the City of Dubrovnik wrote to Giovanna the Queen of Naples: "This city of ours is surrounded by maliciouus Patharens, the greatest enemies of those who follow Catholic religion."[53] And in 1451, the city fathers of Dubrovnik wrote to Pope Nicholas V, the following message: "Dubrovnik is besieged by perfidious Patharens and Manicheans."[54] The family of Columbus most probably came to Dalmatia a generation or two before from the Dalmatian hinterland of Bosnia of Hum (Herzegovina). There, the name Kolonić (Spanish form-de Colon) can still be found today even among the Islamized Croats.

It is interesting to note that though the Patharenic heresy was an anathema in Spain, the Croatian Patharens, true to their Croatian traditions, maintained good relations with Spain, particularly with Aragonese. The champion of the Patharens and staunch Patharen himself was then Stephen, Duke of Herzegovina (1435–1482), a semi-independent ruler, who gave shelter and protection to Good Christians. They were finally expelled from Bosnia in 1459, by his son-in-law King Stephen Thomas (who was also a former Good Christian). Yet, with all this, the Duke Stephen was the principal friend and supporter of Alfonso V, the Magnanimous, King of Aragon and Naples and the grateful Alfonso took this Good Christian under his royal patronage, and confirmed to him on several occasions, particularly in 1454, by Royal charter all his possessions in Herzegovina and Dalmatia. The leader of Good Christians for his part despite his Patharenic religion asked Alfonso to send him several Franciscan friars from Naples, who would work on the conversion to the Catholic faith of his Patharenic subjects! Alfonso sent him a group of Neapolitan Franciscans led by Giovanni de Sallinis Aureis, the Bishop of Ottano in Sardinia.[55]

Did Christopher Columbus come to Naples in the 1450's during this period of close ties between Alfonso of Aragon and the Duke of Herzegovina (who also ruled a large part of Dalmatia), is a matter of conjecture. In the 14th and the 15th century Spain was very much involved in combating heresy in Croatian lands and a number of Spanish missionaries took part. In the 14th century, for example, around 1372, in Bosnia was working on the conversion of Patharens Fray Berengarius, the cousin of King Peter IV of Aragon, while in Columbus' time one of those directing the missionary offensive in Croatian lands against the Patharens was nobody else but Juan de Torquemada, Cardinal of St. Sixt, who in 1461 wrote a book about Bosnian Patharens enumerating their false beliefs.[56]

Under those circumstances it is also understandable, at least in part, that Columbus was somewhat reticent to talk about his past where the Patharenic origin of his family may have come to light, a thing not too helpful in Spain. Columbus' Patharenic origin also may help to explain many aspects of his life which up to this time still remain clouded. For example, his inclination for Greek letters. We have already discussed it. Here it should be noted that the Greco-Croatian alphabet was used exclusively by Good Christians. (In earlier times they used the Glagolitic alphabet which they all also knew).[57]

Equally, Columbus' notorious lust for material goods and money may be also credited to his Patharenic origin. The Patharens in their beginning lived poorly according to the preaching of their religion, but in the 13th century their leaders allied themselves with ruling feudal nobility. In this time "Good Christians" already became merchants, land speculators, bankers and loan-shark operators. With time this sect degenerated morally so much that in 15th century it practically disintegrated by itself, its members easily and spontaneously passed to other religions—Catholic, Islamic and Orthodox.[58] For example in the famous testament of Gost Radin ("Gost" is a high dignitary among Good Christians) which was made in Dubrovnik in 1466, (the Gost being expelled from Bosnia), the refugee Gost, who was supposed to be a poor man, leaves behind him a fortune of 5,650 gold ducats and many other priced possessions. He left it all to his family, his retinue and his friends. He left nothing to his local religious community in Bosnia, nothing to the Church of Good Christians in general.[59]

And when the Turks attacked in 1463, it was the Good Christian's general Radak who surrendered, for a reward, the Royal city of Bobovac, then the capital of Bosnia. (For his reward, fittingly enough, he was thrown into the river by the Turks). When Bosnia was conquered by Sultan Mehmed II, El Fatih, the remaining Good Christians' nobility immediately converted to Islam to conserve their possessions and privileges.

Furthermore, Columbus' equally puzzling relationship with Beatriz Enriquez de Arana which is so much perplexing to his students may be explained by this Croatian-Patharenic hypothesis. It is not of importance if Beatriz was of Converso origin as some believe. The fact remains that she was in Columbus' life more than a mistress. He treated her like a wife and his illegitimate son Fernando which he had with her he treated equally as his older and legitimate son Diego. Fernando was by the will of Columbus next in succession. Columbus gave to Beatriz the initial prize granted by the King and Queen for the one who saw land first 10,000 maravedis which Columbus claimed for himself and snatched away from the poor mariner, Rodrigo de Triana) and she received later a pension from him. He also gave some important posts to her relatives. He ordered his older son and heir Diego to take care of her "as he would of his own mother". In a way Columbus considered Beatriz as his real wife.

The question is: Was Columbus' relationship with her one reflex of his Patharenic origin, a reflex of past customs still in memory?

Croatian Patharens, the so-called Good Christians, did not recognize the sacrament of marriage as Catholics did; their marriage was simply based on a verbal assurance. A Good Christian would take a wife simply under the condition: "as long as You will be good to me and faithful to me".[60]

Beatriz was good and faithful to him and Columbus, as we know, always felt obliged to her. For, it is not surprising that Columbus did not officially marry Beatriz, she may have been an obstacle to his grandiose ambitions because of her low standing, but what is the most surprising is the fact that he never remarried at all. Nobody had particularly discussed this side of

Columbus' enigma, yet, it is absolutely unbelievable! Why did he never remarry? Now, Christopher Columbus was known as a charmer who always had his way with ladies; he loved women. When he came to Portugal, the already middle-aged adventurer had no trouble charming a young Portuguese beauty named Felipa Perestrello e Moniz, who was probably twenty or twenty-five years younger then he, yet she succumbed to his charm instantly. "Felipa was so high on him, she became his wife," explains his son and biographer Fernando. It is said even his mother-in-law was overwhelmed with his charm. He probably had some additional mistresses while in Portugal, maybe even another wife and some more children as he once mentioned himself in one statement which still baffles the researchers. Later in Spain, Columbus, probably now about fifty or more had no trouble whatsoever in conquering a young 20-year-old orphaned beauty, the mentioned Beatriz Enríquez de Arana. And when he went to his voyage of discovery in 1492, he fell deeply in love on the Canary Islands with a young widow named Beatriz de Bobadilla who had inherited the title on the territory of the Island of Gomera. According to some sources Columbus was "deadly" in love with her. He almost abandoned the enterprise of his life for her. This trait—the love for women—is a notorious trait in Columbus' family. His son and heir Diego had numerous mistresses and two illegitimate children from two different girls before he married Dona Maria de Toledo, the niece of the Duke of Alba. His grandson Luis Colon was the same, and this was the only thing in which he distinguished himself; he was once condemned for having had three wives at the same time.

Why, then, did Christopher Columbus never remarry? Regardless of his age he was in a position to choose practically any girl from the leading Spanish families. Beside his natural inclination for beautiful women, a marriage for him in Spain was extremely necessary, indeed imperative. He was a foreigner envied and often attacked and taking into consideration his vanity, his lust for power and glory, his keen sense for political survival, it was absolutely vital for him to remarry and bolster his shaky position in a foreign land through such an alliance. Yet, he never came to this!

On his deathbed it was only Beatriz de Arana he thinks and

cares about. She remained with him, spiritually at least, to the very end:

"And I order You", he addresses himself in his last will to his older son and heir Don Diego," to take care of Beatriz Enriquez the mother of my son Don Fernando and to provide for her so she can live honorably as a person to whom I am in great debt. This must be done to relieve my conscience because this weighs much upon my soul. The reason for it is not licit to write here."[61]

Those are beautiful words and bewildering too. Beatriz Enriquez de Arana definitively was more than a mistress for Christopher Columbus. Was that relationship with her and that consideration for a woman who was both good and faithful to him, an echo of the distant Patharenic origin of this Croatian adventurer? Bartolome de Las Casas in his curious remarks concerning the religion of Columbus, unconciously painted a perfect picture of a Croatian Catholic whose family converted from Patharenic faith maybe one or two generations before: "Seeing himself very weak as a Christian, and certainly he was, he received all the sacraments with much devotion . . . "[62]

No Spaniard of Genoese, particularly an intelligent one like Columbus, could have been a weak Christian Catholic and confused in his understanding of Catholic doctrine, neither could a Converso whose family had been for three or four generations and one full century of time Catholic in rigorously Catholic Genoa have been weak, insecure and confused in those matters. Only a Croatian of Good Christian origin could have exhibited those traits. This is in complete accord with our knowledge of Good Christian converts. The study shows that since their conversion to Roman Catholicism (or better to say their reincorporation) those converts generally continued to exhibit for a few generations considerable weakness and incomplete knowledge of some Catholic dogma before they became hardened Catholics.[63]

That fits the case of Christopher Columbus perfectly. Obviously his family had some connections with Good Christians. This, beside numerous other evidence, is one of the strongest proofs that Columbus was in reality of Croatian extraction.

In the 13th, 14th and 15th centuries—Columbus' time—the

"Good Christians" existed only in Croatian lands. Consequently, only a Croatian could ever have been a Good Christian!

17. Continuing with the religious aspects of the question, further proofs for Columbus' Croatian origin can be found in some items of his testament. Those items are found in the forged testament dated as of February 22, 1498, but are most certainly authentic being inserted into it from the true will Columbus made in 1502, which was never found.

The first item which draws attention is the official signature of the Admiral. After the discovery Columbus began to use a somewhat mysterious signature, said to be Greco-Latin, which he wrote in the following way:

```
            .S.
   .S    .A.    S.
    X      M      Y
      : Xpo    FERENS
```

Numerous attempts have been made to solve this puzzle without success. The proponents of the Converso theory take it for the sign of Kabbala and the shield of David. Jakob Wasserman, the German-Jewish scholar, dismisses the Columbus signature as "some childishness" practiced with the number seven. For his part Samuel E. Morison believes that the signature has some religious meaning.[64] Armando Alvarez Pedroso thinks that the signature contains the initials of his positions and dignities (Señor, Sua Alta Señoria, Excellent, Magnificent, Yllustrious). Salvador de Madariaga says this is doubtful because the signatory does not give titles in the third person, that is to himself.

The latest attempt to resolve this puzzle was made by the Portuguese anthropologist, writer and cryptologist Dr. Augusto Mascarenhas Barreto in his book "O Portugues Cristovao Colombo, Agente Secreto do Rei Dom Joao II". (The Portuguese Christopher Columbus, Secret Agent of the King Dom Joao II). Mascarenhas Barreto brings out strong evidence that Christoforo Colombo the low-born Genoese woolweaver later turned simple seaman existed but he was not the Christopher Columbus we know as the official discoverer of America: Christopher Columbus or Cristobal Colon was another man. The Genoa thesis, says Mascarenhas Barreto, orginated from an error: In a Latin letter from Piero di Manchegna to Queen Isabella where he mentioned

Colonus (Colon) the name was miscopied: Colonus became Columbus.[65] From this small slip of the pen the great historical fraud envolved.[66] Mascarenhas Barreto claims that Colon (Columbus) was Portuguese, half-brother of Diogo, second Duke of Beja and a nephew of the King Dom Joao II of Portugal! He believes that Columbus was sent by his uncle King Joao to Spain as a spy. His task was to distract the attention of the Spanish kings from India, that is to prevent the Spaniards from reaching India by going around Africa as the Portuguese intended. According to this theory the plan called for Columbus to lead the Spaniards on a wild goose chase in the opposite direction—across the Atlantic—by insisting that this was the fastest and shortest route to India.[67] Mascarenhas Barreto also claims "to have decoded" the famous Columbus signature with its peculiar number seven by using "Kabbala mirror methods"—inverting letters by which the Latin "S" became Hebrew "Shin" which means the "Spirit".[68] He also "decoded" that Columbus was an illegitimate son of the Duke of Beja and Isabel da Camara and she was a New Christian, that is, a descendant of the Jews who converted to Catholic religion and, he says, this Catholic Isabel da Camara was the source of Columbus alleged expertise in Hebrew![69]

Mascarenhas Barreto's contention that Christopher Columbus was not Christoforo Colombo, the Genoese woolweaver, certainly seems correct. Anybody who has studied the case without preconceived notion or political considerations has to agree with that: Just too much evidence, not fabricated, exists against the Genoese thesis.[70] But his thesis that Columbus was the son of the Duke of Beja and a nephew of the Portuguese king Joao II sounds rather like a fantasy. Christopher Columbus was clearly a foreigner, penniless and on the move everywhere, in Italy, Spain and Portugal. His extreme mobility his travels from one country to another, his adaptability, his changing of nationality and his constant changing and refashioning of the name according to the country in which he happened to be is in reality, as said before, a striking characteristic of the Croats particularly in those times of Turkish invasions which produced plenty of expatriates and refugees from Croatia wandering in many Western countries. The point is the following: That a Genoese-born who never cares much about his native country and who never goes back not even for a visit is somewhat strange, but that a Croatian expatriate does the same is not. In fact, most of the Coatian expatriates in that time had no place to come back to anyway—most of the country was already conquered by the Turks. Columbus also possessed and inherited nothing in Genoa or any other place in Italy.[71] Similarly, in Portugal Columbus was a foreigner and penniless. He lived some six years at the expense of his wife's family in the houses of his mother-in-law on Porto Santo and Madeira. And he apparently squandered their comfortable wealth. Columbus also possessed nothing and inherited nothing in Portugal—a fact which would be nearly incredible if Columbus was of a royal blood and the nephew of a King. If Columbus was a half-brother of the Duke of Beja, the pro-Spanish conspirator against the King Joao II of Portugal, who Mascarenhas Barreto says Spanish queen Isabella knew all about and if as a such he was sent to Spain as a spy to make the Spanish court believe that he too is pro-Spanish, how did it happen that he arrived in Spain destitute carrying his son Diego without a centavo in his pockets? He begged people for food for his small son!

As for Mascarenhas Barreto's alleged decoding of cryptic seven-letter Columbus signature by "Kabbala mirror methods" and giving it some Hebrew meaning, this has been tried before too. It's a trip into a fantasy-land: Anybody can by playing with those letters and various words and symbols he selects himself arrive at almost any conclusion he wishes. Mascarenhas Barreto says that Columbus used cryptic letters to hide the fact that he descended thru his mother from the Jews who converted to Catholic religion (the New Christians) because the Spanish kings had little sympathy for those New Christians.[72] Nothing is as false as this contention. The notion that Conversos or converted Jews (New Christians) were discriminated against, prevented from success or otherwise persecuted in Spain has also been one of the greatest frauds in history, and was used by some other writers who wanted to prove that Columbus had Jewish connections. Mascarenhas Barreto also uses this same fraudulent argument to arrive at a similar conclusion. The plain truth, however, was that the New Christians who were sincere converts (or had appearance of sincere converts) not only were never persecuted but had all the doors open for themselves in Spain. In fact, the Jewish converts, the New Christians almost owned Spain. For generations and centuries Spain was governed by New Christians who held all kind of positions in the Spanish Realm. And this was also true in Columbus' time when those Conversos dominated completely the Court of Spain.[73] The entire household of Queen Isabella was Jewish: the converted Jews were in charge of all affairs of the Court of Spain—political, economic, military, as well as ecclesiastic. Both confessors and confidants of Queen Isabella who exercised an immense influence over her were of Jewish ancestry. Even the Church of Spain itself, the most rigorous and most Catholic in Europe, was dominated by New Christians. Cardinal Juan de Torquemada, for example, was a New Christian, so was the Inquisitor General, himself, Cardinal Tomas de Torquemada, according to numerous sources. The Church of Aragon, in particular, was totally entrusted into the hands of converted Jews.[74]

Thus no obstacles whatsoever were present in Spain to anyone who has converted to the Catholic religion even if this conversion happened only a day before. According to contemporary thinking and practice in Spain, the Catholic religion made all inhabitants of the Spanish Kingdom equal regardless of their racial or ethnic origin.[75] And when the New World was discovered and the Royal office which was to oversee and govern the new lands was created in Seville, converted Jews were placed there too in prominent positions. Furthermore, it is a well-known fact that Columbus himself was accompanied on his voyages to New World by several royal commissioners who were converted Jews or New Christians—some of them the most recent converts.

Thus it is false and it is a distortion of history to say that Columbus hid his origin and his identity so that it would not come out that he had certain New Christian (Jewish) connections in his family tree which, in any case, would have been only partial and remote. Quite the contrary, being a New Christian was a sure ticket for success in Spain in those times. It is very well known that some powerful New Christians in the Court of Spain, like Gabriel Sanchez and Luis de Santangel, in fact, helped Columbus. They would not have been there, in those positions, if success in Spain was precluded for New Christians!

Therefore, all this talk that Columbus used cryptic words and cryptic signature to hide certain connections of his family with Jews—many in Spain, including the royal family, had such connections—is also great historical nonsense.

Columbus, for his part, had no connection with New Christians and, evidently, had a certain dislike for them. This he proved once when he physically attacked and savagely beat up the Royal Commissioner, Ximeno de Breviesca, who was a converted Jew. The Sovereigns of Spain were not pleased with this incident and were so furious at their Admiral that Columbus was forced to apologize to the King and Queen (so much for Mascarenhas Barreto's contention that the King and Queen of Spain had no sympathy for New Christians!)

Returning to Colubus' much discussed signature, it, despite its enigmatic form, appears as yet another proof of Columbus' Croatian origin. It is really hard to guess what Columbus meant with this signature, that is with the part preceding his signature. However, I believe that both Pedroso and Morison were partially right: it seems to be an autotitulation with religious invocation. But, Columbus surely meant much higher titles and honors included in his signature (higher than Señor and Sua Señoria), particularly if we assume that he was a Croatian who came thru Venice. He may have modeled at least a part of his signature from the title of the Doge of Venice. And why not? He was not an ordinary magnate, he was a vassal only to the King of Spain, beyond that he was on his own: Viceroy, Governor General and Admiral by privileges not only for life but hereditary in perpetuity.

I believe the first four letters which were stressed by dots mean: "Signatura (de) Sua Altessa Serenissima', while the three remaining letters without the dots may be some religious invocation, very probably that of the Holy Family which was very popular and frequent in Dalmatia (XMY—Hristos, Maria i Yosip or Christ, Mary and Joseph) and of which Columbus was incidentally also very fond. Bartolome de Las Casas also noted that Columbus always wrote on his letter or any writings the invocation: "Iesus cum Maria sit nobis in via" (Jesus with Mary be with us on our voyage). I do not know about the others but this, incidentally, is the traditional, centuries old invocation of Croatian mariners and travelers from Adriatic to this day.

As for "Serenissimo" this was the word always used in addressing the Doge of Venice by everyone and, especially by Dalmatian Croats, and Columbus used this word frequently while referring to the King and Queen of Spain which means he was habituated to it. We may assume the Croatian adventurer considered himself in his new position just about as much "serenissimo" as the Doge of Venice, who also originally was a vassal (of the Byzantine Empire) but, obviously, he did not dare to autotitulate himself with such title openly knowing, of course, that this could have been considered by the Crown of Spain, that is by the King and the Queen, as an affront, that almost put him at their level, so he wrote down the initials of his self-given title and left it to posterity to guess . . . After all he was some sort of serenissimo. His rank was equal to that of the Admiral of Castile, a person of royal blood. (Uncle of King Ferdinand). That those first four letters probably indicate an autotitulation is attested by three facts. For one, the signature which Columbus always used and which he ordered for his heirs to use always, obviously was important for him and must have some meaning, it cannot be simply dismissed as some childishness. The mysterious letters always preceded his signature which means those letters are related to it. Thus it follows that this part of his signature denotes an autotitulation. Secondly, he began to use such a signature only after the discovery, that is, after he became, effectively, the hereditary Viceroy and Admiral, and thirdly, he ordered in his will that this must be the official signature of every one of his heirs who bears the title of Viceroy and Admiral and only the Viceroy and Admiral signs like that, not his other relatives.

But the most interesting part of Columbus' enigmatic signature is the last part—the signature itself. It is generally described as a Greco-Latin signature in which the first part of Columbus' given name is written in Greek letters—"Xpo" (Hristo), the last part in Latin—"Ferens". Here it must be pointed out that it is virtually impossible that Christoforo Colombo the Genoese woolweaver knew the Greek language and knew how to write it. Furthermore, he never really used any typical Greek letters.

The only letters which are said to be Greek in his signature were the "X" and the "p". Of course, those letters are also found in the Latin alphabet. But Columbus did use those letters in the first part of his signature in a Greco-Eastern sense: Thus "X" stands for "H" (for Hristo or Hristos which means Christ) while "p" is used for the letter "r". But that does not mean that Columbus knew Greek. Those two letters are found also in various (Greek-based) Cyrillic alphabets on the Balkan peninsula. Those letters are also found in the same sense in the Croatian version of the Cyrillic alphabet.[76] In the 14th and 15th centuries that Cyrillic alphabet was the one most used, particularly by Croatian Good Christians. In the beginning they used the Glagolitic alphabet which they all also knew but from the 13th to the 16th century it was Croatian Cyrillic.[77] The fact that Columbus used the word Hristos (in Cyrillic form) also confirms directly, his Croatian origin. Hristos is how the Greek-Orthodox refer to Jesus Christ. In Italy and in all Catholic Europe there is no Hristos, except in Croatia, where both, Catholics and Patharens (Good Christians) used the words, Hristos, Hrist (Hristo in combination) for Christ and wrote it in Croatian Cyrillic letters as Columbus did.

This was the source of Columbus' alleged Greco-Latin signature which in reality was a Croato-Latin signature. This is confirmed furthermore by the fact that Columbus also knew the other Croatian particular (and original) national alphabet, the Glagolitic one, which he undoubtedly used in those mysterious "letters of unknown characters" to his brother Bartolome on Hispaniola which his enemies intercepted and sent to the King and Queen in Spain.[78] And, of course, Columbus knew and wrote in Latin letters, that is, he knew and used three different alphabets. This proves decisively that he was a Croatian: In Columbus' time the Croatian people were the only people in Europe who possessed concurrently three alphabets, Cyrillic, Glagolitic and Latin, and all three were widely in use.

This is substantiated also by that same Columbus' cryptic signature related to number seven. The much-discussed Columbus' attraction to number seven was always an enigma which baffled many historians. No one was able to find any cogent explanation for that peculiarity of Columbus which was, by the way, one of his many oddities. Naturally, the explanation is impossible if we suppose that Columbus was Christoforo Colombo, Genoese. On the other hand if we suppose that Columbus was Croatian the solution is easy and immediate. In the first place it must be noted that the number seven is a "special" Croatian number which appears constantly in the history of Croatian people. Before their final migration to the Adriatic in 7th century the Croats lived in Central Europe beyond the Carpathian Mountains in the territory of today's Southern Poland, part of the Ukraine as well as in parts of Bohemia and Slovakia. This was called White or Great Croatia and its capital was Hrvat (Croat) which stood on the site of today's Cracow.[79] In 626, the majority of Croats migrated to the Adriatic and settled in the ancient Roman provinces of Dalmatia, Panonia and Illyricum where they founded the Kingdom of the Croats.[80] This they did with the consent of the Byzantine Empire and at the invitation of the Byzantine emperor Heraclius. The Byzantine Empire was then in a very precarious situation. By 626, the mighty Avars overran and conquered the entire Balkan peninsula and laid siege on Constantinople itself while their Persian allies besieged the city from the sea. In that moment of extreme peril the Emperor Heraclius turned to the Croats in White Croatia for help. He invited them to come South and promised them all the lands they could wrest away from the Avars.[81]

According to written and oral history the Croats came to the Adriatic divided into seven tribes. They were led by seven siblings—five brothers, Klukas, Lobel, Muhlo, Kosentzes and Hrvat and two sisters, Tuga and Buga.[82] Each led one of the tribes. They organized seven autonomous provinces or federal states. Each one was ruled by a Ban (equivalent to a Viceroy). There were seven bans under one elected common king. In a Cartulary of Supetar which originated about the year 1098, and which is conserved in a somewhat worn out transcript from around 1300, it says: "In past times in the Kingdom of the Croats the following custom existed: There were seven bans which elected the king in Croatia when one would die without children: Ban of Croatia (Metropolitan) first, Ban of Bosnia second, Ban of Slavonia third, Ban of Požega (East Slavonia) fourth, Ban of Podravia (probably Podramia or Hum) fifth, Ban of Albania (Dioclea or Red Croatia) sixth and Ban of Sriem seventh.[83] Number seven thus was an important number for the Croats and it appears often later in their history. But, much more than that, in the lives of the neo-Manichean Croatian Good Christians to which Columbus' family undoubtedly had certain connections in the past and to which about 30% of Croatians had connections in 14th and 15th century, the number seven was not just their special number: For Good Christians the number seven was their sacred number.[84] The Patharenic neo-Manichean Good Christians took that number for a sacred one also from the Revelation of the Apostle St. John the Divine.[85]

The entire life of a Good Christian was related to number seven and so were all his daily activities.[86] For the neo-Manichean Good Christians there were seven churches in Asia, there were seven stars, seven golden candelabras, seven trumpets, seven thunderbolts, seven horns, seven wounds. There were seven Spirits who prayed before God day and night. There were seven chalices which contained the prayers of the holy ones.[87]

Every Good Christian was required to pray seven times a day and seven times at night. Every time he was to say seven Pater Nosters (Our Fathers).[88]

Besides that for every occasion the Good Christians were required to say seven "Our Fathers". For certain special occasions, like, for example, for the very important dispensation of solace the Good Christians were required to say "dobla" that is to say twice the seven Our Fathers. Also if a Good Christian was to ride a horse he was to say seven Our Fathers twice.[89]

Taking into consideration all that was said previously about the subject I believe it is self-evident that Christopher Columbus was in reality a crafty and ingenious Croatian adventurer. There is just too much evidence for it; all the facts we know about Columbus, for sure, fit in. Everything, absolutely everything can be explained and squared with this Croatian hypothesis and all that cannot be product of a mere coincidence.

18. But, still, this is not all. There is more to it. His order of succession, for example. It is significant that Columbus excluded his female descendants from succeeding him: "This mayorazgo (entail-estate) must in no way be inherited by one woman, unless

here or on the other side of the world a man of my true lineage cannot be found who calls himself and his ancestors de Colon."[90]

This arrangement of succession in his testament is purely and distinctively Croatian in its form and content. It is in perfect accord with Croatian customs and juridical conceptions of the time: A woman does not inherit titles nor possessions unless there is not a single male relative alive. This rule was a typical rule in all Croatian regions. It was always categorically emphasized as Columbus does it himself.

Even the Venetians followed this rule in their acquired part of Dalmatia to conform with the traditional laws of their Croatian subjects. The Republic of St. Mark did not want to upset the existing customs and juridical formulas of Dalmatian Croats in its hard- and costly-won Dalmatia. Thus, the Venetians were the ones who usually conformed. For example, in 1459, the Venetian Mayor of Zadar asked from Croatian authorities (in Free Croatia) what the Croatian law and customs say regarding succession and inheritance of property so he could act according to it in regard to local Croatian inhabitants in Zadar and its surroundings. He received from Michael Živković, the Vice-Ban of Croatia the following reply; "All possessions of all noblemen from the twelve tribes of the Kingdom of Croatia pass to the male offspring . . . The female child has no right to the part of patrimonial possession, but must be given a dowry from movable property when she marries . . . "[91]

Always only the male descendants are the heirs of their fathers and legal holders of patrimonial possessions, titles and ruling rights. And if a man does not have a son, the title and the ruling right passes on to the next male relative closest to him (brother, nephew, first cousin etc.)

This old Croatian law about succession, strictly thru the male line, is often stressed in Croatian medieval documents. For example, in an agreement made between Stephen Kotromanić, the Ban of Bosnia, and the City of Dubrovnik in 1333, it says: "The Ban and his sons and his descendants in male line . . . for me, my sons, and my descendants in male line until the end of this world". Count Radoslav Pavlović in 1432, says: "and the rest of them by blood in the male line". The City of Dubrovnik conferring its citizenship on Count Vukac Hranić in 1405, states:

"the Lord Count Vukac (brother) of the Lord Duke Sandal and their children, grandchildren and greatgrandchildren in male line".[92]

Columbus' order of succession thus appears, strikingly, as a Croatian medieval legal formula. Its meaning, wordings and style is so typically Croatian that one cannot escape the impressions that it could have been formulated only by a Croatian:

"I name my dear son Don Diego for my heir . . . and if he will not have a male heir of his own, the succession passes to my son Don Fernando, and in the same way, not having a male heir himself, it will be inherited by Don Bartolome, my brother . . . and if he will not have a male heir either, then my other brother will inherit it and it has to extend like this from one relative to other, the closest to my line and so it must be forever. And a woman must not inherit it, unless there is no man left of our lineage" . . .[93]

This order of succession, contrary to the customs of Castile in which he lived and died, is made exclusively in accordance with traditional customs and laws of the Croats.

Furthermore, in the final analysis, Columbus' real national origin comes to light when compared to two of his known contemporaries whose cases were virtually identical to his own: One was an obscure man about whose past, equally, very little is known and who became, also under somewhat dim circumstances, a known mariner; the other one was also of unknown past and origin who became late in Columbus' life, suddenly, his right hand man, literally a member of his own family, the one which, with the exception of Columbus' own brothers and sons, was the closest man to him on this earth. Their extremely intriguing, interesting and particular cases, convincingly, point out Columbus' true national origin:

19. The mystery and the origin of Christopher Columbus thus cannot be discussed without mentioning still another similar case, that of his contemporary fellow navigator John Cabot who in 1497 sailed to the New World under the English flag, trying to emulate Columbus, because the parallel among the two is striking. Departing from Bristol with the ship "Matthew" he reached Newfoundland in June of the same year and then promptly returned to England to announce his discovery. The

question posed here is, just as in the case of Columbus: Who was that mysterious sailor called John Cabot?

Italian, of course, we are told, and this is generally accepted, just as is Columbus' origin. The noted American author Samuel E. Morison says Cabot was "probably" a Genoese.[94] However, he does not have any proof for such a statement nor has anyone else: The birthplace, national origin and the past early life of John Cabot is equally mysterious and unknown—even more so than that of Columbus. Even his age and his exact name, again just as in the case of Columbus, is unknown and is given in many forms by many writers and contemporary documents. Absolutely no trace has been found of Cabot and his family in Genoa or anywhere else in Italy. Only two facts are known about John Cabot. First, that he was a citizen of Venice, hence, he was called the Venetian. But he was only a naturalized Venetian, not Venetian-born. In Venice there is a document from the Venetian senate, dated in 1476, in which it states that the privileges of citizenship of Venice are granted to Giovanni Caboto for having resided fifteen years in the city according to custom. Thus Cabot lived in Venice, for sure, from 1461 to 1476. He also married a Venetian woman and had three sons, Luigi, Sebastian and Sancio, all born in Venice. His second son, Sebastian, later also became a famous navigator and was Piloto Mayor (Chief Pilot) of Spain. The second fact known about John Cabot is that he was a merchant in Venice buying and selling real estate, but he was, probably originally a sea merchant and had commercial transactions in Adriatic and Mediterranean and maybe, just maybe, in the Near East. He said to Raimondo di Soncino, the envoy of the Duke of Milan that he was once in Mecca, which was an obvious lie. Cabot liked to boast about his exploits, which he never realized and often went beyond the limits of the truth (another similarity with Columbus!), for no Christian could have entered the Holy City of Islam. Next we find certain Venetian called Johan Cabot Montecalunya residing between 1490 and 1493 in Valencia in Spain where he tried unsuccessfully to interest King Ferdinand in the project of building a jetty. No doubt, this was the same John Cabot. Here in Spain he saw, in 1493, the triumphant return of Columbus from his first voyage to the New World and got the idea to emulate him. It seems quite certain that Cabot previously knew Columbus and was well aware of his true origin. In 1496, John Cabot presented himself at Court in London to the English king Henry VII, and proposed to do for him what Columbuss did for the Spanish kings—to cross the Atlantic and reach the "Indies" . . . This is just about everything what is known of John Cabot and from such scanty informations it is hard to figure out who John Cabot really was.

To determine the original nationality of Cabot two facts are certain which can serve as the starting point: 1.) There are no data which show that Cabot was born anywhere in Italy and 2.) He was a naturalized citizen of Venice and very fond of his adopted city. Looking now at those two facts and taking into consideration all that was previously said about Croats and their relations with Italians, the only logical and rational solution would be to presume that he was Croatian-born, particularly when we find him in Venice. The Republic of St. Mark had a large stake in the Croatian pie; it was already nearly a century that Venetians owned a large part of Croatian coast of Dalmatia, and this being so, from where can a man in this time come whose roots in Italy do not exist and who lives in Venice, if not from Venetian Dalmatia or some place in that vicinity? Owing to the generally poor knowledge of Croatian history in the West and of close ethnic and other links between Croats and Italians such a possibility has never been raised before. It must be considered now, for there is no other acceptable alternative, unless somebody presents some concrete proofs of John Cabot's birthplace somewhere in Italy. The non-Italian origin of Cabot, i. e. his Croatian rather than Italian extraction is suggested by his very own name which was regularly misspelled in Italy. Even in Venice, of whom Cabot was a naturalized citizen and where he spent some twenty-three years, his name sounded unfamiliar and un-Italian.

He was called Caboto, Cabota, Cabot, Gabote, Gabota, Gabot, Babate, Talbot, Gaboto, Cavotta etc. Even in his adopted city, Venice, where he spent twenty-three years of his life, where he married and was naturalized, nobody really knew his name for certain. In a document of 1476, granting him the right of citizenship, the Venetian Senate calls him "Caboto"; however, the Venetian Lorenzo Pasqualigo in a letter from London in 1497, calls him "Zuam Talbot" (which may have been also a misprint for "Calbot"), while the same Venetian Senate later in 1551, calls his son, Sebastian, "Gaboto"!

The same confusion, the same enigma that we see in the parallel case of Christopher Columbus!

The logical supposition thus should be that both men in question, Columbus and Cabot, were just "transitory Italians"; that is to say, somewhat Italianized Croats from the Croatian Adriatic littoral which was so influenced by Italy and often intermixed with Italians and most of which was ruled thru centuries by Venice. Only this seems to explain the unquestionable discrepancies of existing data, both Spanish and Italian, the discrepancies arousing obviously from their "imperfect" Italian origin. They were, in reality, two Croatians who came originally thru Venice.

Now, Columbus and Cabot both belong among the most prominent men of the past. Their achievements and discoveries, at least those which have been credited to them, had the most profound impact in the history of human race. Certainly, we know the names of all the prominent Italians from Columbus' time and of those before—we have no problem with that. Furthermore we know too, that all those prominent Italians in history also knew what their names were and naturally knew how to write them. This, however, was not the case of Columbus and Cabot: We have their names given, sometime even by themselves, in several different versions. Neither they, themselves, nor others were certain how their true names should really look! Absolutely an extraordinary, unique case in history which poses the inevitable question: What kind of Italians and supposed Genoese were they? Really, when the question is viewed calmly, rationally and most of all logically it does appear extremely questionable that the two mariners, Columbus and Cabot, could have been from Genoa when a) They, themselves, never said that they were Genoese; b) They never did anything for Genoa; c) They never even visited Genoa; d) Their brothers and sons also never said that they were Genoese, never visited Genoa and never did anything for Genoa; e) They did not care at all for Genoa and one of them (Columbus) even fought against Genoa; f) They knew Venice, resided in Venice, had a profound love for Venice, Genoa's enemy, and one of them (Cabot) made himself a naturalized citizen of Venice, unless we revise our concept of basic logic and accept the proposition that one and one makes three.

Fortunately, the case of Cabot, as well as that of Columbus, can now be judged on much more than logic and common sense. The question of nationality of Cabot and, by extension, that of Columbus, two of the most celebrated and controversial cases in history, can now be resolved almost beyond doubt.

Fortunately, the definitive evidence which proves that John Cabot was really Croatian-born does exist.

The first clue is given by the same John Cabot when he left Venice for Spain (like Columbus did long before). Between 1490 and 1493, he was in Valencia in Spain where he tried to build a jetty with royal backing, but King Ferdinand was not interested in the project of this obscure man from Venice who now called himself by a rather peculiar un-Venetian and un-Italian name—Johan Cabot Montecalunia! This, of course, is very interesting and very significant. By using such a name Cabot plainly revealed what was obvious—that he was not Italian-born. No Italian would change his name Caboto to Cabot in Spain because the form Coboto is perfectly good in Spanish while Cabot is not Spanish. Also, in Spain, Cabot ceased to be Giovanni which was his first name in Venice. And, more interestingly, he did not become Juan (in Spain) as it would have been expected. Instead he used the name, Johan, which is German for John, or, more probably he derived it from Latin—Johannes. But the wholly unexpected fact that Cabot did not use in Spain either the Italian or the Spanish form for both of his names shows that he was not born in Italy (nor, of course in Spain).

But, the third added part of his name—Montecalunia or Monte Calunya—which Cabot invented and fashioned in Spain, is the most interesting of all. Obviously it comes from something in his life's background. Fashioned in Spain it sounds Spanish but is only partly Spanish. Of course, "Monte" means mount, hill, mountain, but what is Calunia or Calunya? That word, however, has Croatian connotations: In Dalmatia the old word "calun" ("kalun")—still in use today—means cannon. Therefore, "Montecalunia" in English translation would mean "Mount Cannon" or "Cannon Hill" which makes sense.

John Cabot's real Croatian name was undoubtedly, Cabota (Kabota), a name under which he was also known. Such names with the same suffix ("-ota") are characteristic and purely Croatian names, especially in those times, names like, Bakota, Cikota, Krmpota, Bota, Dorota, Kažota, Imota, Kastriota, Dobrota, Palmota, Lerota, Subota, Markota, Pinota, Rebota, Pierota, Relota, Sakota, Rodota,Mikota, Surota, Dragota, Vukota, Šegota, Glavota, Babota as well as Gabota, another name under which John Cabot was also known. Such names were even more numerous in the Middle Ages and in John Cabot's time, but in subsequent centuries many of those names tended to acquire the more pronounced Slavic suffix "-otić" (otich) in place of "-ota" so today also some of those names exist in both versions, the older and the newer one like, for example, Bakota and Bakotić, Vukota and Vukotić, Šegota and Šegotić etc. (All Croatian names today which end in "-otić" ended sometime before in "-ota").

As to Cabot's first name John (Giovanni, Ivan) it should be noted that he was also referred to as Zoanne (Zuan) which is a popular Adriatic version of the name Ivan (Giovanni). The Croatian version of it, Zvane (or Zvan) was also popularly used among the Croats along the Adriatic in those times and it is still widely used today.[95]

Most probably Zvane Caboto-Cabota hailed from that part of Dalmatia (Southern) which still belonged to the Kingdom of Croatia: The City of Dubrovnik or its surroundings. In those parts some similar names can be found like, for example, Caboga, which incidentally, is the name of a noted trading and patrician family from Dubrovnik, much known among the nobility of Dalmatia. The Cabogas were the typical urban Croatian family which thru business, cultural and traditional ties had a strong Italian orientation. Like most of the better families from Croatian Dalmatia, the Cabogas were bilingual, using even more Italian than Croatian. In fact, they were very much Italianized. They also wrote some literary works, too, strictly in Italian.[96]

Furthermore, this family, even much before John Cabot, had maintained for generations, extensive relations with Venice. In Croatian medieval folk literature there even exists a popular old tale which narrates, in a funny way, how one Caboga, a merchant from Dubrovnik, outsmarted the Doge of Venice.[97]

The Cabogas did their commercial dealings as much in Venice as they did in Dubrovnik proper, which may also explain why John Cabot, himself, settled in Venice in the first place.

Evidently, the family of John Cabot resembles that of Caboga in everything including in name. Both names, Caboga and Cabota (Caboto) are purely Croatian names similarly constructed. Kaboga (Caboga) is also sometime given in more pronounced Coatian (Slavic) form, Kabozić. In literal English translation this means "As (of) God" (Ka + Boga). Kabota (Cabota), on the other hand, means "As (of) Once" (Ka + Bota). Bota (which means "once" or "one time") comes also in the more pronounced Croatian-Slavic form, Botić, which is a known Croatian name—thus Kabotić. This name (Kabotić) in the Italian form reads Caboto, the name under which Cabot was most frequently mentioned. (Incidently, Bota, is also the name of another well known seafaring family from the territory of the Republic of Dubrovnik!)

There can hardly be a doubt that Giovanni Caboto-Cabota (John Cabot) was originally a Croatian.

Speaking of John Cabot, we know nothing of his relations with Dubrovnik, not because such relations did not exist, but because we know very little, almost nothing about John Cabot himself. However, his most famous son, the Venetian-born Sebestian, himself a noted navigator maintained a known link with countrymen of his origin. As in the case of Columbus, the best friend and person of absolute confidence of Sebastian Cabot was a certain Croatian, a man exactly from Dubrovnik!

When Sebastian Cabot undertook his well-known intrigue with Venice, when he proposed to leave the service of Spain of which he was the Chief Pilot and return to Venice (with all the Spanish navigational secrets, of course) it was a Croatian whom he chose as a man of his total confidence for this delicate and extremely dangerous mission. That was Hieronimo de Marin di Bucignolo, a Croatian nobleman from Dubrovnik.[98] Bucignolo, as it was usual among the Croats in Dalmatia, is the Italianized form of Croatian name Bucinjić or Buconjić very well known and numerous, them and today, in Dubrovnik and in the surrounding region, particularly in Herzegovina. Di Marin or de Marino means the son of Marin. This fact is very important; the intrigue was a dangerous play which may have cost Cabot his life and what appears of outmost significance, when the chips were down, was that Sebastian Cabot, though born and raised in Venice, did not confide this mission to some Venetian, though there were numerous Venetians in Spain, nor did he confide it to any other Italian (Spain was as usual full of Italians from any part of Italy), but to a Croatian, a man from Dubrovnik (Ragusa), which points out that this was probably the area from where the Cabots originally came. Sebastian Cabot, undoubtedly, was well aware of it. Psychologically speaking, as is well known, when a person is confronted with crucial decision, when one has to take a gamble in which everything is at stake, including his own life, one goes instinctively by nature with his own kind as must have been the case with Sebastian Cabot. This seems to be the only possible explanation why he chose a Croatian for this critical mission.

The proposal of Cabot brought to Venice by his Croatian envoy was accepted with enthusiasm by the Council of Ten, and an order was issued to the treasurer of Venice to present a gift of 20 ducats to Lord Hieronimo di Marin for his good service.[99] Only then was the Venetian ambassador in Spain, Gaspar Contarini informed of the affair by the despatch of the Council of Ten sent from Venice on September 27, 1522, with instruction to contact Cabot. Contarini succeeded in arranging a meeting in his place in which the matter of Cabot's defection was discussed. The Venetian ambassador in a letter to the Senate of Venice described Cabot as being a frightened man who begged him to keep the matter secret because his life depended on it. Sebastian Cabot told Contarini that he had a great friendship with this man from Dubrovnik to whom he opened his heart and confided to him to take care of the entire affair and instructed him to disclose it, in total secrecy, only to the members of Venetian Council of Ten, which the Croatian swore on the sacrament to do.

Cabot's intentions of defecting from Spain never materialized. His enthusiasm cooled. Obviously, the reason for it was the geographical impossibility of the Republic of St. Mark to break out of the Adriatic and the Mediterranean through the strait of Gibraltar. The maritime power of Venice, once so formidable, was no match for that of Spain and she was confined by the Spanish Armada to the Adriatic. Her chances of competing on the open seas against Spain and Portugal who dominated the globe were equal to zero.

However, the Croatian was working hard for Cabot in Venice. Not only did he handle the project of Cabot's defection, he handled also all his personal affairs, his and those of his family. In a letter from Venice dated April 28th, 1523, the Croatian urged Cabot again, "for the love I have for You," as he expressed himself, to return as soon as possible to the city of St. Mark where all his desires would materialize. He proded Cabot to hasten his return to be in time to recover the dowry or inheritance of either his mother or of his aunt or uncle who was very old.

It is very interesting that Bucignolo used here the unusual and unknown word "ameda" (et ameda) which the researchers could not decipher. They only assume that it probably means "mother". But, the word "ameda" (amedja) exists in Croatian. This is, in fact, a word of Turkish origin which by then (in 1523), after a century of Turkish onslaught and occupation came into use in Croatia. It is still in use today and it means an "uncle", also an "aunt". The fact that Bucignolo used such a word proves that he knew the Cabot family was of Croatian extraction and expected that Sebastian Cabot, though Venetian-born, would know the meaning of this word from his father and his father's family and relatives.

To return to the elder Cabot, his original Croatian nationality is further indicated by the fact that he attracted many Croatian sailors to England. The Venetian Lorenzo Pasqualigo wrote from London to his brothers in Venice that many Venetians are there and are going with Cabot. Those Venetians were for the most part, if not exclusively, the Venetian Croats from Dalmatia who always constituted the great majority of sailors on all Venetian ships.[100] The very appearance of Cabot and those Venetian-Croatian sailors in England was nothing extraordinary. Venetian ships with predominantly Croatian crew as well as the ships and sailors from Croatia proper, particularly from

Dubrovnik—"Argosy" in the English language—frequented England even before John Cabot. Recently, the tombs of Croatian sailors have been found in Southern England dating from 1491. That is five years before Cabot set foot on English soil.

The second Cabot expedition in 1498, was an English enterprise, more or less only in name. In reality it was an international enterprise. So apparently was his first, somewhat controversial voyage. There were few Englishmen on those voyages. In fact, no name of a single Englishman who took part in those expeditions is known! On his first voyage with the ship Matthew there were only 18 crew members. No names are known. Only what is known is that it included one Burgundian passenger and an Italian barber from Castiglione near Genoa. On his second voyage maybe up to 300 people took part. The great majority of them were the Croats from Venetian-occupied Dalmatia and there were some of other nationalities too. There was one known Italian, the Milanese cleric Giovanni Antonio de Carbonariis and even one known Spaniard, the notorious monk, Father Buil, who participated in the second Spanish voyage of Columbus to the New World (1493–1496), where he acquired a reputation as a troublemaker.

The second voyage of John Cabot in 1498 was a total fiasco. Of the five ships which undertook the expedition one (that with Father Buil aboard) became disabled because of a storm and had to sail, in distress, to an Irish port and then, shortly after, returned to Bristol, while the other four with John Cabot aboard were lost without a trace. However, Cabot or some survivors of his expedition reached the American mainland down South toward Cape Hatteras in North Carolina.[101] Cabot's surviving sailors, who were mainly Croats or, probably, exclusively Croats, mixed there with Indians producing thus a new Indian tribe called Croatoan (Croatan) Indians. And an island near Hatteras on which they originally found refuge became known as the Croatoan Island. Their descendants were found later in 1584, by Sir Walter Raleigh in his noted voyage to America which ended in the creation of the ill-fated Virginia colony.

That the ancestors of some of those Croatian Indians around Cape Hatteras were really Croats is beyond any doubt. This is confirmed not only by their clear and correct name, but also by the look of some of those Indians. Both English chroniclers in the expeditions of Raleigh and Grenville in 1584–1586, Arthur Barlowe and John White, describe some of those Indians as having certain European features and being of lighter, yellowish color and reported seeing Indian children with very fine chestnut and auburn hair.[102]

This is unquestionable proof that the ancestors of some of those Indians were indeed of European, Croatian ancestry, and the survivors of the second expedition of John Cabot. On his voyage Sir Walter Raleigh also found a definitive, direct proof that those Indians were of Croatian ancestry. Describing his find, Sir Walter Raleigh, who established the short-lived English colony in North Carolina on July 20, 1584, wrote: 'one of the trees . . . near the entrance had its bark peeled off, and five feet from the ground, the word CROATOAN was engraved . . .'[103] Croato, Croata, Croatoan, Croatan this is how the Croats were called then and throughout the history everywhere in Europe and in their own Latin documents (Latin was the official language in Croatia until 1847), and so they are generally called today too. The forms Croatian and Croatoans were particularly used in those times in the archives in Rome and Italy as well as in some parts of Germany, especially in Frankfurt the great mercantile center of Europe.[104]

Therefore, the Croatians were there long before Raleigh. According to information the local Indians had, some of those white men later built some kind of ship and took off with the aim of returning to pick-up the others, but they were never seen again. They never made it. Some of those left on the island later carved that word "Croatoan" maybe as much as fifty years after the shipwreck and before dying. It could be that those Croats who left the island in their own manufactured ship perished in a storm right along the coast of North Carolina where the remnants of a certain ship were found later. Or maybe that sunken ship was part of the original fleet of John Cabot.

Still in 1714, the British historian Lawson estimated that the remnants of this ship were there at least twenty years before the arrival of the English (Raleigh). Writing about the ship, Hamilton McMillan in 1880 states, "Croatoan Indians have traditions which are tied to the individuals, the owners of the destroyed ships from the past . . ."[105] Croatoan (Croatan) Indians later left the Croatoan Island and moved into the interior of North Carolina where they intermixed further with other Indians, yet they preserved their distinctive Croatoan name under which they are officially known today (Croatan Indians). They also preserved their traditions as a people of mixed Indian and white blood. They claim to be the descendants of early native tribes and white settlers. They live today in various parts of North Carolina, but mostly in Robeson. They are officially recognized as people of mixed White and Indian origin.[106] The researchers who studied the remnants of those Croatan Indians in North Carolina have found traces of certain Croatian customs and claim that Croatan Indians still use several Croatian words like, for example, when they cut grass or grain, they say "pokosi", a distinct Croatian word (verb) which exactly matches the Croatian expression.

The research about those fascinating Croatian Indians is really only at its beginnings and the future will probably bring some interesting results. When and how those Croatoan Indians originated has long been a matter of some discussion. It as proposed that sometime around 1540, a few ships left Dubrovnik carrying with them a number of Croatian refugees who had fled to Dubrovnik from the then Turkish occupied Bosnia and Herzegovina in search of asylum, and those ships were transporting them to the New World to be resettled there. One or more of those ships sank in a storm along the coast of North Carolina and that's how the Croatian Indians originated. But this theory is flawed, and appears impossible. First, there is nothing in historical sources and archives suggesting that something like that ever originated from Dubrovnik. Secondly, it is unlikely that those ships would be bringing the refugees to be resettled that far North in wilderness in a totally unexplored territory for which even the Spaniards did not much care. The ships from Dubrovnik navigated where the Spanish ships navigated and if they were carrying future colonists they would have more likely sailed much more South to those parts of the New World which the Spaniards already explored, conquered and colonized or were in process of colonizing, and where the Spanish administration already existed. Furthermore, the Croatian settlement on Croatoan Island near Hatteras predates the year 1540. It is much older than that. The Croatoan Indians the English saw there had no knowledge nor recollections, that is no first hand knowledge about their ancestors except that they were White men. They knew no name of anyone, not even a first name of any one of them. The scanty information they gave was second hand though those White men would have been still living among the Indian men of their own generation. If those alleged castaways from Dubrovnik were the founders of a Croatian colony near Hatteras in the 1540's, then their oldest sons and daughters would have been only 30 to 40 years old when the English found them. In that case they would have known many things about their fathers, if not from their fathers directly, then from their mothers and other relatives. And if their fathers were Europeans they would have had a strongly European appearance and many of them would have been, no doubt, able to pass entirely for Europeans. But this was not the case; the Croatoan Indians on Croatoan Island, although obviously a mixed breed, were, in 1584, just that, Indians, that is predominantly and mainly Indian-looking. What Sir Walter Raleigh was seeing on Croatoan Island in 1584 was not a first generation of European offspring in America; those were not the sons and daughters of Europeans. What Raleigh and other English explorers were looking at were the Indianized, some second but chiefly the third and fourth generations of European offspring.

This bring us neatly back to the turn of the century and to John Cabot. There can hardly be a doubt that the ancestors and founders of those Croatoan Indians near Hatteras were the Croatian sailors from Venetian Dalmatia in the ill-fated expedition of John Cabot in 1498, which is generally believed to have ended right there.[107] Therefore, those Croats from John Cabot's expedition were the forerunners of the British Empire in America and of the United States of America—the first Americans. That is, the first European settlers in today's U.S.A.

To figure out the origin of those mysterious Croatoan Indians in North Carolina really should not have been a problem so insurmountable, but as it was previously pointed out, most of Western historians, particularly the English-speaking ones, no matter how renowned they are, generally know very little about the history of Croatia and even less about the particular and intricate relations of the Croatian people with the Italians and especially the Venetians, throughout history. And in those times the Croatians from the Northern shores of Adriatic, the Croatians from North and Central Dalmatia, from the islands of Primorje and from Istria generally counted as Venetians, and were, politically, Venetians because they were the subjects of Venice, those territories being then part of Venice.

Thus when the Venetian Lorenzo Pasqualigo reports home from London that "many Venetians" are going with Cabot, for such historians this is it, they take those Venetians literally. They cannot even imagine that those "many Venetians" or at least part of those "many Venetians" could have been, in fact, "other Venetians" that is, the Croatian subjects of Venice from Dalmatia and other parts, all owned by Venice, though that was the case and always was the case, especially when it concerns the sailors, because throughout the centuries the Croats always made up the majority of sailors and naval personnel on Venetian ships.

By the way, like that of Cabot, the Columbus case itself also suffers from that same misunderstanding: when the researchers following some strong evidence indicating that Columbus may have come in reality from Venice investigated there and found nothing much, no one ever got to pose the simple and the most logical question: Well, if not from Venice proper, then maybe from Venetian Dalmatia?

Today, increasingly, this appears to have been exactly the case! But the most intriguing and at the same time the most important remark about John Cabot is that of the Spanish ambassadors to England, Ruy Gonzalez de Puebla and Pedro de Ayala, who sent a despatch from London in 1498 to the Catholic sovereigns in which they reported that the King of England is sending "another Genoese like Columbus" in search of the Islands across the Ocean!

Now, John Cabot was not a Genoese, there is nothing belonging to John Cabot in Genoa. He came to England as a Venetian citizen, he called himself always a Venetian, was called by others, officially and unofficially a Venetian, was surrounded by Venetians (mainly Venetian Croats), was very proud of Venice and though in the service of England he carried with him the flag of Venice and planted it in the newly discovered land of

America along with the English. How could he have been from Genoa, the traditional, centuries-old rival and enemy of Venice?

In a "Letter-Patent" granted to John Cabot and his sons, the king of England Henry VII, says: "to our well-beloved John Cabottus, citizen of Venice . . . " The same thing he says in the second "Letter Patent" accorded to John Cabot. William Purchas, the Lord Mayor of London, mentions Cabot twice as Venetian, as does Raimondo di Soncino, the envoy of the Duke of Milan, who reports on a certain Venetian, Zoanne Caboto who was sent to discover new lands by the King of England. The Venetian, Lorenzo Pasqualigo, wrote from London in August of 1497 to his brothers, Alvise and Francesco, about "our Venetian" who discovered new lands and raised there also the flag of St. Mark because he is a Venetian.

How then did it come about that Spanish ambassadors mistook John Cabot for a Genoese? The rumor that Cabot was a Genoese was noticed only in England. That rumor originated probably and inadvertently from Cabot himself who in all probability personally knew Columbus while he was residing in Spain or, maybe, he even knew him from their early years in Venice where Columbus once also resided for a certain period.[108] But Cabot was misunderstood: What Cabot hinted in England was undoubtedly that he was of the same nationality as Columbus. Since Columbus was generally passing for a Genoese, both Spanish ambassadors consequently wrote home about Cabot as "another Genoese like Columbus". Taking into consideration all that was said here about Columbus and the Cabots, the despatches of Spanish ambassadors, Ruy Gonzalez de Puebla and Pedro de Ayala, supply another, though indirect, yet powerful support for our thesis that Christopher Columbus indeed was of Croatian nationality. The main point of their letters and their importance for history is that they linked Cabot and Columbus as being of the same national origin. This helps to resolve the enigma: Cabot was not at all Genoese so Columbus could not have been either. Though the Ambassadors, unaware of the real origin of both navigators, in their (honest) ignorance have described them as "Genoese", their identification of them as being of the same national background may be precious for future history. In light of the latest investigations the historical meaning of their despatches should really read: "John Cabot another Croatian like Columbus."

Salvador de Madariaga wisely remarks that certain mentions of John Cabot as "Genoese" diminish the value of many documents which referred to Columbus as "Genoese", because Cabot came from Venice.[109]

Indirectly speaking, that Columbus was a Croatian and not a Genoese is also confirmed by the attitude the Sovereigns of Spain had in Columbus' case. They were surely the only ones who knew the truth about the origin of their Admiral as well as the truth about the discovery, yet, they never, officially or unofficially, identified him as a Genoese, neither him nor his two brothers. Contrary to the familiar custom in those times by which the nationality of a man or the province, city or place of his birth was regularly added after his name such as, for example, "Portugues", "Frenchman", "Venetian", "Genoese", "Florentine", "Calabres", "of Candia", "of Sicily" and so on, in the case of Columbus his nationality, his country or province of origin or his place of birth is never mentioned.[110]

He was always referred only as "extranjero" (Foreigner) with no national description and this was the official and absolute rule of the Court of Spain. Other Genoese were Genoese, Columbus never.[111] The King and Queen of Spain always resolutely refused to mention Columbus as Genoese and when that letter of their ambassadors from London arrived telling of Cabot as "another Genoese like Columbus", the King Ferdinand, avoiding the word "Genoese", replied to his ambassador, Gonzalez de Puebla, that he (the Ambassador) is talking about someone like Colon (Columbus) who went there to propose to the king of England a similar enterprise. As far as the sovereigns of Spain were concerned, the word "Genoese" did not apply to their Admiral.[112]

That someone like Colon was, of course, John Cabot. Evidently, all indications point out that Cabot and Columbus were, both, just two ingenious Croatian adventurers who had nothing to do with Genoa. Just two Croatians, Italianized to some degree, it may be added, as were in those times many Croatians from Dalmatia, and almost all who went over to Italy, who shrewdly and skillfully seized the historical opportunities of their times, the times of great discoveries, to gain immortality. And the starting point of their amazing adventures which were to take them across the great ocean was, undoubtedly, that famous Venetian "Riva dei Schiavoni" (The Coast of the Croats) or "Riva od Hrvata" as the Croats called it themselves. This was the starting point for the foreign adventures of thousands and thousands of Dalmatian Croats almost throughout their history, among them another great adventurer of Croatian extraction and the idol of many, Marco Polo, whose fantastic travels announced the era of great discoveries.

20. Finally, an intriguing and extremely important bit of evidence suggesting the Croatian origin of Columbus is represented by that venerable figure of Father Gaspar Gorricio, a Carthusian monk from the famed Monastery of Las Cuevas in Seville. Columbus met Fray Gaspar late in his life, in 1498, six years after his first voyage to the New World. Yet, that Carthusian monk of equally obscure origin immediately became the right hand man of Columbus and his most intimate friend. In fact, he became a kind of senior member of Columbus' own family.

Gorricio was a confidant and an adviser to the official Discoverer, as well as his archivist and treasurer. He kept in his cell in the Monastery of Las Cuevas all the personal papers of Admiral, his privileges and his treasure. He collaborated with the Admiral in his "Book of Prophecies" which was put together mainly by the material Fray Gaspar supplied to Columbus and in which the repeated references were made to St. Hieronymus the Patron Saint of Dalmatia and of Adriatic Croats! He tended to the affairs of his brothers too. Since Gorricio was a monk, Columbus went to the trouble of obtaining a brief from the Holy See in Rome to permit Gorricio to come out of the monastery, when needed, to take care of the affairs of Admiral and his family. Gorricio was a tutor to the sons of Columbus and acted as their father in the absense of the Admiral. Of the extraordinary relationship between Gorricio and Columbus family the best account is given by Admiral himself in his farewell letter to his older son Diego before embarking on his third expedition to the "Indies": "My dear son," wrote Columbus, "I am leaving You in my place . . . all my privileges and personal papers are left with Fray Gaspar (Gorricio) as well as an inventory of my properties . . . I order You, under pain of disobedience that in all important matters You follow the advice of Father Gaspar; everything must be done with Fray Gaspar's acquiescence and advice and not any other way, and work to secure for him a brief from His Holiness so he can take care of my affairs . . . "

After the death of Columbus, Gorricio asked and obtained permission from his order to attend to the affairs of the sons of the Admiral and defend their rights. In 1507, Gorricio, personally, traveled to Rome to ask a brief from the Pontiff himself in this matter. His voyage to Rome coincided with that of of Bartolome Colon, the brother of the late Admiral. Pope Julius II, conceded him the desired brief and Gorricio, upon his return to Spain, moved to the Royal Court to be in better position to defend with more efficacy the rights of his two young protégés.

In April of 1509, Diego Colon, the "Second Admiral", asked the Pope's permission for Don Gaspar to take care of his own testament. In May of 1509, Diego made his own will naming Fray Gaspar the effective executor of his testament. In 1514, Gorricio was also a redactor of the testament of Columbus' youngest brother Diego and upon his death in the following year was one of the executors of his will together with his brother Francisco Gorricio, and assisted in his burial in the Chapel of Santa Ana.

In his cell in the Monastery of Las Cuevas Gorricio probably kept all official documents of Columbus until his death and after that the documents of his son the "Second Admiral" were deposited there and were still there in 1523. Columbus' son even built a luxurious residence near Seville to be close to Don Gaspar. Father Gorricio died in 1515, apparently in advanced age. He, however, survived all three Columbus brothers.

Here, another all important question is also posed: Who was Gaspar Gorricio? What was his real ethnic background?

There are only few notes left on Father Gorricio and his family. All that is noted is that he came from some place called "Novaria". In 1495, before he met Columbus, a religious work "Contemplations over a Rosary", written by Gorricio was published in Seville. In the beginning of the book it is stated: "This is the beginning of the first part of contemplations over a Rosary of Our Sovereign Virgin Lady and Mother of God, Sancta Maria, arranged by Don Gaspar Gozrico de Novaria, the monk of Cartuxa". In the Columbian Library in Seville an epistle of Don Gaspar is preserved in which it is written: "The epistle of Don Gaspar Gozricio de Novaria, the monk of Cartuxa to his brothers Francisco Gozricio and Melchor Gozricio in which he commissions them to have the present work printed and published". One of his brothers, Melchior Gorricio, was a professional printing contractor and publisher who published several books of a religious nature in Latin, among them "Missale Mixtum alme ecclesie toletane" in 1499, in which, on the next to last page is written: "Impresum jasu ac impensis nobilis Melchioris Gorricii de Novaria".[113]

Beside this, there exists one document dated October 3, 1515, in which Fray Gaspar Gorricio is mentioned as a tutor and guardian of the person and properties of his nephew Antonio Gorricio de Novara, the son and heir of the late Francisco Gorricio de Novara and his wife Ines de Arriaga.

The above stated is just about all that is known of Gorricio and his family. From the last mentioned document in which it is said that the young Antonio Gorricio and his late father are "de Novara" instead of "de Novaria", most of the researchers believe that the family was originally from Novarra in Northern Italy.[114]

However, it is certain that Gorricio was not an Italian. In regard to his origin some observations are in order.

It must be noted, in the first place, the striking similarity between the case of Gorricio and that of Columbus. In substance both cases are identical. Like those of Columbus, the origins of Gorricio are no less uncertain and obscure, only a few scarce lines on him and his family exist. Nothing is really known of his ethnic background and, like that of Columbus (and Cabot), his name, equally, is enigmatic and comes in four or five different variations! Even Gorricio, himself, was unsure how his name was supposed to look and he wrote it, himself, in three different forms! What kind of Italian was he?

As for the city of Novarra being the birthplace of Gorricio this is also uncertain despite that document from 1515, in which one member of his family is mentioned as "Antonio Gorricio de Novara". Fray Gaspar and his brothers wrote their name "de

Novaria". Now, it does not necessarily mean that this must be Novarra in Italy. The document of 1515 was made in Spain by a Spanish notary and it mentions the young Antonio Gorricio who was born in Spain from a Spanish mother and his father who was dead. It seems likely that the Spanish notary, not being sure about "Novaria", concluded it must be Novarra in Italy and wrote down "de Novara".

However, in substance it is of little importance where Gorricio was born. He may have well been born in Novarra, though it is more likely that he was only living there with his family for a short time, if at all. One idea recurs—he must have been a Croatian, at least by his father's side. He may have found himself in Novarra for some time, not an extraordinary occurrence with countless Croats always traveling in Italy or living there permanently. And if it was really Novarra it should be noted that Fray Gaspar and his brothers strangely enough, wrote this name in the corrupted form "Novaria". Now, this indicates strongly that the Gorricio family was in reality Croatian, for such a linguistic corruption of the name Novarra into "Novaria" fits perfectly with linquistic spirit and medieval forms of Croatian language, while it can hardly be imagined that the brothers, Italian-born and Novarra-born, would call their native city in such a corrupted form. (The Spaniards, also, never call Novarra "Novaria"!)

But for Gorricio's Croatian origin there is one more, literally irrefutable proof which so far has been overlooked by the researchers. It is his name—Gorricio. This is purely a Croatian name. Gorricio derives from the Groatian word "Gorica" or "Gorice", thus Gorricio means "of Gorica". In the Croatian language this name exists, also, as Gorički or Goričić (Goricius). Gorica or Gorice means "Little Forest", also a "Forested Hill" from which numerous same or similar names derive. When this Croatian name Goričić (Goricius) is given a Spanish form it reads Gorricio, exactly as the name of Fray Gaspar is generally written, while the Italian form of this Croatian name is Gorizio. (Compare, for example, the pronunciation of the city of Gorica on Italo-Slovenian border, the scene of fierce fighting in World War I. This city has the original Croatian and Slovenian name of Gorica, but the Italians call it Gorizia).

Thus, Gaspar Gorricio, regardless of the place of his birth, appears definitively of Croatian extraction. The Croatian origin of Gorricio is even further confirmed by the fact that no trace of the Gorricio family has been found in Novarra nor, for that matter, anywhere else in Italy. Furthermore, the Gorricios belonged to nobility. In all four books published by Melchior Gorricio it is stressed that the family is noble. Now, if in those times an authentic noble Italian family with the name Gorricio (Gorizio) existed in Novarra it would be virtually impossible that no trace of it can now be found.

But, Gorricio, in fact, was not his real name. It was only one refashioned, that is, Latinized, to look more Spanish, though even as such it remained purely Croatian.

Of particular interest and importance thus is also how Fray Gaspar, himself, wrote his name. In fact the real name of Gorricio family was Gozrić (Gozrich) or Gozričić or something very close to that. In "Contemplations over a Rosary" printed in 1495, his name is given as "Gozricio" and "Gozrico". In an epistle which he wrote to his two brothers Don Gaspar writes his and his brothers' name, also, three times as "Gozricio". Now, this is another irrefutable proof that Gorricio was a Croatian who obviously had a trouble adjusting his name to the Latinized form of the Italian or the Spanish. No Italian, particularly a highly educated man, a literate man like Father Gorricio would write his name as "Gozricio" and "Gozrico" with the two consonants "zr" together, for such a usage as "zr", without a vowel in between, does not exist in the Italian language (nor in Spanish), while in Croatian the "zr" is common and comes in countless words. This detail, of summary importance, somehow has also completely escaped the eyes of the researchers despite the impossibility of the linguistic form. This came about from the fact that the world was, for a long time and for a variety of reasons mentioned before, so saturated with the notion that Columbus was an Italian that most people, including most of the historians, can't even imagine that something or somebody around him could have been anything but Italian. This despite the fact that in Columbus' life—the one we know for sure, roughly from 1480, until his death in 1506, there were no Italians and absolutely nothing Italian around him. (He never even spoke Italian!)

Yet, this detail is nothing short of sensational because it gives to the whole Columbus case an entirely new twist. It proves conclusively that Gorricio-Gozricio was of Croatian origin. But it does more than that. By association it implies strongly that Columbus was also of the same origin.

Without doubt, Gorricio was for many reasons the person in which the family of Columbus confided the most. The motives for such extraordinary trust and mutual friendship formed in a foreign country can only spring from a common ethnic background. The historians agree on that.[115] Obviously, the nationality of Gaspar Gorricio-Gozricio contains a clue to Columbus' own national origin. Now, in view of Gorricio's certain Croatian origin and the extraordinary relationship he had with Columbus' family one cannot avoid the logical conclusion or, at the very least, the strong possibility that the national origin of Christopher Columbus was, most probably, the same as that of Gaspar Gorricio.[116]

In summary, there can be little doubt that the final determination of the exact ethnical background of Gaspar Gorricio-Gozricio, as well as that of John Cabot, would give us a key to Columbus own ethnical origin. The researchers of the future should concentrate mainly on those two men whose enigmatic early lives and cloudy origin resemble and parallel so much that of Columbus that it can be hardly construed as a mere coincidence.

Along with the discovery of Columbus' origin, the real truth about the discovery of the New World will also emerge.[117]

# Notes

## PART I.
## THE ENIGMA
## OF CHRISTOPHER COLUMBUS

1. See pages 43–85, Part III.
2. " . . . sin salir de ella tiempo que se haya de contar"—LOS QUA-TRO VIAJES DEL ALMIRANTE Y SU TESTAMENTO, edit. I. Anzaotegui, Collecion Austral, Madrid, 1964, p. 213.
3. Tornate a El y conoce ya tu yerro: su misericordia es infinita. Tu vejez no impedira a toda cosa grande; muchas heredades tienen El grandisimas. Abraham pasaba de cien anos cuando engendr, a Isaac, ni Sara era moza" Ibid. p. 196.
4. Salvador de Madariaga—Christopher Columbus, F. Ungar publ., New York 1967, P. 40.
5. Indications are that Columbus himself helped squander her inheritance.
6. See text of the letter in—Salvador de Ma dariaga—Op. Cit. p. 424.
7. Ibid. pp. 423–424.
8. Ramon Menendez Pidal—LA LENGUA DE CRISTOBAL COLON, Col. Austral, Madrid 1958, pp. 23–25.
9. Ibid. pp. 23–25.
10. Salvador de Madariaga—Op. Cit. p. 50. Text on the passus on page 434, note 14, also, Ramon Menendez Pidal—Op. Cit. p. 24.
11. Ramon Menendez Pidal—Op. Cit. p. 25.
12. "Y vi todo el Levante y Poniente, que hice por ir al camino de Septentrion, que es Inglaterra, y he andado la Guinea . . . "—LOS QUATRO VIAJES DEL ALMIRANTE . . . p. 98.
13. Antonio Ballesteros y Beretta—CRISTOBAL COLON Y EL DES-CUBRIMIENTO DE AMERICA, Barcelona 1945, pp. 507–509.
14. See pages 100–106.
15. LOS QUATRO VIAJES DEL ALMIRANTE . . . p. 140.
16. " . . . estas tierras estan con Veragua como . . . Pisa con Vene-cia"—Ibid. p. 192.
17. Actually, Columbus exhibits some poor knowledge of Genoese names and expressions. He refers, casually, for example, to the names of many Genoese in their corrupted Spanish-Portuguese forms as they were called on the Iberian peninsula. He does it

even for persons whom he must have known personally in Genoa, if he was indeed a Genoese, like for example for the Fieschi family whom he calls "Flisco" (The Fieschi family was a political power in Genoa and the Colombos from Genoa were said to have been her partisans).

Obviously, whatever Genoese names, words and expressions, particularly nautical terms, Columbus used, he learned them all on the Iberian peninsula, in Portugal and Spain. That is why those names and words often appear in incorrect corrupted Hispanic forms. "Genoese", therefore, was never the maternal language of Columbus: He never used it, never wrote in it, never spoke in it with anybody, not even with his own brothers and never thought in it. Spanish, not Italian "Genoese" was his habitual language of thinking and expression. This fact has been proven beyond any doubt even by those who, like Ramon Menendez Pidal, for example, continued to adhere to the old notion that Columbus was the former Genoese wool carder. And this clearly is visible in all his writings. Even his Latin was Hispanized: Whenever his Latin went wrong it always went the Spanish way. This too has been proven over and over again.

A publican and a woolworker born in Genoa and raised in Genoa who subsequently marries and settles in Portugal cannot think in Spanish!

18. For this particular point see: Salvador de Madariaga—Op. Cit. pp. 428–430, Chapter IV, Note I.
19. Salvador de Madariaga—Op. Cit. pp. 49–50.
20. " . . . en cuya compania estuvo y anduvo mucho tiempo"—Bartolome de Las Casas—HISTORIA DE LAS INDIAS, Mexico 1965, p. 34.
21. " . . . no dice sino que, segun todos af irman, este Cristobal era Genoves de nacion . . . "—Ibid. p. 28.
22. Salvador de Madariaga—Op. Cit. p. 424, note 8.
23. Ibid. p. 34.
24. See here Part IV. pp. 58–151.

# PART II.
## RESOLVING THE ENIGMA:
## COLUMBUS' ROLE IN THE DISCOVERY
## OF AMERICA

1. Samuel E. Morison—ADMIRAL OF THE OCEAN SEA, Boston 1942, p. 62.
2. Ynca Garcilasso de la Vega—ROYAL COMMENTARIES OF THE INCAS, vol. I., NEW York, p. 26. (no year)
3. Bartolome de Las Casas—HISTORIA DE LAS INDIAS, vol. I., Mexico 1965, pp. 70–72.
4. Jose de Acosta—HISTORIA NATURAL Y MORAL DE LAS INDIAS, Mexico-Buenos Aires 1962, p. 52.
5. " . . . sua mesma carta de marear, onde tinha demarcada a terra"—Simon de Vasconcellos—CHRONICA DA COMPANIA DE JESUS DO BRASIL E DO QUE OBRAVAO SEUS FILEOS NESTA PARTE DO NOVO MUNDO, Lisbon 1663, vol. I., pp. 3–7.
F. Ximeno de Sandoval—CRISTOBAL COLON, Madrid 1963, p. 314.
6. Felipe Ximeno de Sandoval—CRISTOBAL COLON, Madrid 1963, p. 92.
7. Bartolome de Las Casas—Op. Cit. pp. 35–36.
8. Salvador de Madariaga—Op. Cit. pp. 84–87.
9. In fact it is not even certain that the original letter of Toscanelli to the Canon of Lisbon and the much discussed map of Toscanelli ever existed. There are three views among historians as to what concerns the "Toscanelli correspondence": some, mainly those from the past believed everything was authentic, others contended the letter to the Canon of Lisbon is genuine while that to Columbus is a forgery and the third view is that everything is a forgery. The last seems to be the truth: Nothing at all exists which would prove that Toscanelli wrote anything in this matter to anyone in 1474.
His alleged letter to the Canon of Lisbon does not exist.
10. Salvador de Madariaga—Op. Cit. pp. 169–171.
11. Columbus, seemingly, was an acquaintance of Sanchez, an old friend as Las Casas himself notes.
12. " . . . pero, porque segun tengo entendido, que quando determino buscar un principe cristiano que le ayudase e hiciese espaldas ya el tenia certitumbre que habia de descubrir tierras y gentes en ellas, como si en ellas personalmente hubiera estado (de lo qual cierto yo no dudo)"—Bartolome de Las Casas—Op. Cit. p. 37.

13. Salvador de Madariaga—Op. Cit. pp. 127–128.
14. Ibid. p. 128.
15. Ibid. pp. 128, 132.
16. Ibid. p. 128.
17. See here Part IV. pp. 58–151.

# PART III.

## POLITICAL ASPECTS OF THE DISCOVERY OF AMERICA THROUGHOUT HISTORY AND TODAY

1. Howard K. Beale—THEODORE ROOSEVELT AND THE RISE OF AMERICA TO WORLD POWER, Collier Books, New York 1965, p. 138.
2. Ibid. pp. 85–158.
3. J. Patrick McHenry—A SHORT HISTORY OF MEXICO, Dolphin Books, Garden City 1962, p. 59.
4. Charles F. Lummis—LOS EXPLORADORES ESPANOLES DEL SIGLO XVI, Col. Austral, Madrid 1960, p. 77.
5. Ibid. p. 79.
6. William H. Prescott—THE CONQUEST OF PERU, Mentor Books, with new notes and a new summary of civil war by Victor W. von Hagen, New York 1961, pp. 394–395, note 22.
7. Ibid. pp. 394–395, note 22.
8. Marianne Mahn-Lot   COLUMBUS, New York 1961, p. 66.

## PART IV.
## THE REAL ETHNIC BACKGROUND OF CHRISTOPHER COLUMBUS; A NEW HYPOTHESIS

1. Bare Poparić—HRVATI U VENECIJI, Hrvatska Smotra V, Zagreb 1937, pp. 289–296.
2. Dominik Mandić—CRVENA HRVATSKA, Chicago-Ziral, second ed. 1972, p. 262. Also note 28, p. 266.
3. He may have been even born on Korčula, though some others give his family as being originally from the Croatiian town of Šibenik in Northern Dalmatia.
4. Ferdo Šišić—PREGLED POVIJESTI HRVATSKOG NARODA, Zagreb 1962, p. 364.
5. Marin Bego—HRVATI KAO POMORCI, Drina No. 3–4, Madrid 1964, pp. 105–106.
6. See pages 131–135.
7. See here Part II, pp. 28 41.
8. Ferdo Šišić—Op. Cit. p. 483.
9. Aleksandar Veljić—KOLUMBOVI MORNARI, Studio No. 928, Zagreb 1982, pp. 66–67.
10. Ibid. p. 67.
11. Ibid. p. 67.
12. B. Kojić-R. Barbalić—ILUSTRIRANA POVIJEST JADRANSKOG POMORSTVA, Zagreb 1975, p. 77.
13. " . . . (y estan tambien ciertas raices de arboles en el mar, que segun la desta Espanola se llaman mangles), estaban llenos de infinitas ostias . . . son blancas de dentro . . . y muy sabrosas, no saladas sino dulces y que han de menester alguna sal, y dice que no saben si nacen en nacaras, dondequiera que nazcan, son, dice, finisimas y las horadan como dentro en Venecia"—Bartolome de Las Casas—HISTORIA DE LAS INDIAS, vol. II, Mexico 1965, pp. 20–21.
14. See: Vinko Lozovina—DALMACIJA U HRVATSKOJ KNJIZEVNOSTI, Split 1936.
15. Ferdo Šišić—Op. Cit. p. 364.
16. Ibid. pp. 381–383.
17. " . . . mas de que se solia llamar antes que llegase al estado que llego, Cristobal Columbo de Terra-rubia y lo mismo su hermano Bartolome Colon"—Bartolome de Las Casas—HISTORIA DE LAS INDIAS, vol. I, Mexico 1965, p. 28.
18. Ibid. p. 154.
19. It was proposed that "Terra Rubea" may have originated from the

name of a noble Catalan family, Monros, with whom some families with the name Colom had relations (so Columbo de Tierra-rubia equals Colom de Monros!). But this cannot be so, this is yet another fantastic deduction. "De Terra Rubea" as Las Casas and Columbus' own son Fernando give it, is not another added name of Columbus. It clearly designates the country, province or region from which the Columbus brothers came. Besides, the Catalan word "Monros" does not mean "Red Land" (Tierra Rubia), but "Red World".

20. With the description "de Terra Rubea" ("from the Red Land"), Columbus and his brother Bartolome also may have meant their native country as a whole, which would be, historically, correct. Beside having Red Croatia (South Croatia) and numerous other Red Lands throughout the country the description "Red Land" (Terra Rubea) is applicable also to all of Croatia. Red is the Croatian national color brought all the way from the ancient Iran, red is the main color of the Croatian national flag, of its national coat-of-arms (the checkered old Iranian chessboard), of all its folk costumes. Also, that distinctive old Iranian cap, round and flat on top, "crvenkapa", also called "Croatian cap" (Hrvatka) is red. In general, that is, Terra Rubea and Croatia are, historically, about synonymous.

21. Dominik Mandić—ETNIČKA POVIJEST BOSNE I HERCEGOVINE, (Bosna i Hercegovina, vol. III.), Rome 1967, p. 350.

22. Christoforo Colombo, the Genoese woolweaver could not have had any meaningfful contacts and conversations with the people of the Greek-Orthodox faith and their religious leaders and scholars. In his life one cannot find place for such contacts and knowledge. He spent all his life in Genoa, Portugal, Spain and America. There were no Greek-Orthodox' in those parts at all.

23. WADHA EL AMERI, in "Hrvatski Književni List", No. II, Zagreb 1969, pp. 4, 10

24. Lavoslav Glesinger—JEVREJI I HRVATI U ARAPSKOJ ŠPANIJI, "Jevrejski Almanah", Belgrade 1955–1956,—"Hrvatski Književni List", No II, Zagreb 1969, pp. 4, 10, Cit.

25. Salvador de Madariaga—CHRISTIPHER COLUMBUS, F. Ungar Publ., New York 1967, pp. 57–62.

26. Ibid. p. 60.

27. See here pages 62–71.

28. KUŠANI, in "Hrvatski Književni List", No. 15, Zagreb 1969, p. 4.

29. Bartolome de Las Casas—Op. Cit. p. 28.

30. Samuel E. Morison—ADMIRAL OF THE OCEAN SEA, Boston 1942, p. 364.
31. In Croatia even some noble families whose names derive from the Latin or Croatian word "dove" like Columbus' does do not, necessarily, have a dove featured in their coat-of-arms. Of such known Croatian families, like Columbarich, Columbini, Colombini, Columbani and Golubić, the first named, Columbarich, has the dove in both versions of its coat-of-arms (in second one with an olive branch in its beak), while the others do not have it. Those families are the branches of the well-known Hektorović family from the Island of Hvar, whose distinguished member, Petar Hektorović (1487–1572) is one of the greatest poets in Croatian history.

   From the same line are also the following families: Hettoreo, Anzoli, Eterović, Ettorei, Barbis, Canavelli, Giaxa, Jakša, Jakšić, Griffico, Piretić and Petris. Instead of a dove they all have, including Columbini, Colombini, Columbani and Golubić a cow's head featured in their coat-of-arms.—See: Adam S. Eterovich—CROATIAN & DALMATIAN COATS OF ARMS, Ragusan Press, Palo Alto, California 1978.
32. Even Columbus' contention which he once made that he descended from some illustrious Roman family, allegedly named Colon, would not go against the Croatian hypothesis. Witness the case of this Frankopan family. In those historical times of Humanism and Renaissance such claims were common.

   Everyone then tended to turn toward antiquity and toward Rome. The Croats (who because of it became generally known as Illyrians) did the same. The Croats were, in fact, the ones who produced the greatest Latin poet since the fall of the Roman Empire, Ivan Česmički, who was a contemporary of Columbus. He was educated, as usual, in Italy and was later the Bishop of Zagreb and a Ban (Viceoy) of Slavonia (Northern or Pannonian Croatia). Of course, as a Latin poet he is better known to the world as Iannus Pannonius. In Columbus' time the habit of linking one's origin to some illustious Roman family was also a notorious trend among Croatian nobility. In the beginning of the 15th century, for example, Count Nikola of Krk, the Ban of Croatia, decided that his family descended from the ancient Roman princier family, Frangipani, and since his time this premier Croatian family was always called Frangipani (Frankapan or Frankopan in Croatian version) until 1671, when the executioner's sword cut off the head of its last member, the Marquis Francis Christopher Frankapan in Wiener Neustadt in Austria. And other leading Croatian family, that of Šubić Zrinski, also pretended to descend from the Sulspiciuses of Rome. Equally, the Counts or princes from Krbava claimed Roman ancestry and said they were descended from the Torquatus family of Rome. The last member of this family, Ivan Karlović of Krbava, the Ban of Croatia and a contemporary of Columbus (died in 1531), did not call himself anything else but Torquatus. (Incidently, there was in those time one Croatian noble family which in reality descended directly from those Torquatuses of Rome. This was the family of Count Posedarić, well known in Senj).

How it was perfectly normal for a Croatian in Columbus time to be considered of Roman ancestry is attested by Columbus' contemporary and his own frequent source of references, the same Pope Pius II, who casually commented about a Croatian nobleman, one of the ambassadors of Matthias I, King of Hungary and Croatia: . . . "They were . . . Stephen, Count of Croatia, a Roman of the Frangipani family which once produced the most holy Pope Gregory" . . . ("Memoirs of Renaissance Pope, the Commentaries of Pius II," Edit. by Leona C. Gabel, George Allen & Unwin, London 1960, p. 122).

33. See pages 72–80.
34. Ramon Menendez Pidal—LA LENGUA DE CRISTOBAL COLON, Col. Austral, Madrid 1958, p. II.
35. " . . . viendole despusicion de otra tierra o reino ageno a su lengua" . . . Ibid. p. II.
36. Salvador de Madariaga–CHRISTOPHER COLUMBUS, F. Ungar publ., New York 1967, p. 349.
37. See pages 88–89.
38. Columbus was himself a lay member of the Franciscan order. This is very significant: the Franciscan order was by far the most popular and the most numerous in Croatian lands. In Dalmatia, Bosnia and Herzegovina the Franciscans were almost the only Catholic clergy. They were in the forefront of the battle against the Patharenic heresy, in resistance to the Turks and were the principal custodians of Croatian cultural heritage and among other the sole guardians and propagators of St. Hieronymus' cult and traditions.
39. Marin Tadin—UN NOUVEL EXEMPLAIRE DU CAREME ATTRIBUE A SAINT BERNARDIN DE SIENNE, in "Madićev Zbornik" (Collectanea Mandić), Rome 1965, pp. 178–182.
40. Ibid. p. 183.
41. Ibid. pp. 178–185.

42. See pages 107–111.
43. "El qual viendose muy debilitado, como cristiano, cierto que era, rescibio con mucha devocion todos los Sanctos Sacramentos"—Bartolome de Las Casas—Op. Cit. Vol. II., p. 329.
44. Salvador de Madariaga—Op. Cit. p. 57.
45. LOS QUATRO VIAJES DEL ALMIRANTE . . . p. 73.
46. Salvador de Madariaga—Op. Cit. p. 219.
47. Dominik Mandić—BOGOMILSKA CRKVA BOSANSKIH KRSTJANA (Bosna i Hercegovina, vol. II), edit. Croatian Hist. Institute, Chicago 1962, pp. 424–425.
48. Ibid. pp. 185, 249–250.
49. Leo Petrović—KRŠĆANI BOSANSKE CRKVE, Sarajevo 1953. Oton Knezović—POVIEST HRVATA, vol. I, Madrid 1961, p. 308.
50. Little is known about those neo-Manichean Patharenic heretics who called themselves Good Christians until the second part of 12th century when this sect began to spread. In 1199, the Archbishop of Split, Bernard, chased away a number of them from around Split and Trogir in Central Dalmatia. They found shelter in Bosnia where the local Ban (Viceroy) Kulin protected them and where the Patharenic population was already numerous by this time. Kulin, himself, was a good Catholic, but the Good Christians deceived him by insisting that they were too, except that they were just "misunderstood" Catholics! In 1200, Pope Innocent III wrote to Emeric, king of Hungary and Croatia complaining about the laxity of Ban Kulin and of the spreading of Patharenism in Bosnia and asked the King to eradicate those heretics from his domains. In 1203, the Papal envoy, Cardinal Giovanni de Casamare, went to Bosnia to try to make some order there. He called a people's assembly to Bilino Polje (Bilino Field) near Zenica, which Ban Kulin, the Bosnian aritocracy and the common people, Catholic and Patharens attended. There the famous document the "Confession of Bosnian Christians" was issued. At this meeting the Good Christians convinced the Papal envoy that they were just that—Good Christians; that is, good Catholics who want to be good Catholics, the only difference being their lack of understanding of the dogmas of the Catholic church. At that the Roman cardinal thought that the problem has been resolved and gave them his approval and benediction. But like Ban Kulin before, Giovanni de Casamare was deceived too. Now armed with official Papal approval, this sect spread rapidly throughout Bosnia and beyond, and very soon the Vatican and the Hungaro-Croatian kings realized they had a real problem. In the 1230's Bela III, (IV),

king of Hungary and Croatia and his brother Koloman, the Regent of Croatia, personally led an expedition against the Patharens in Bosnia and the surrounding regions with the aim of eradicating them once and for ever. Especially harsh on them was the Croatian regent Koloman which "with the sword and with the flame" succeeded in forcing them to publicly renounce their heresy. Koloman thought the problem has been solved, but he too was wrong. After this experience the tenacious Good Christians adopted a new tactic: When the royal army was in their regions they would all act like Catholics, and swear that they were good catholics but after the royal army departed their catholicism also departed. Since then this notorious game was played over and ever again. The strongest and final effort to return those Good Christians back to Catholicism was made in 15th century during the lifetime of Columbus. The attempt had the assistance off Rome and the Western church, especially the Spanish one. This was during the reign in Bosnia of king Tvrdko II (1421–1443), and of his successor, Stephen Thomas (1443–1461). The latter was himself a Good Christian and though a son of a former king he lived for a long time in poverty as a simple peasant in accordance with the teachings of Good Christians. He also took for a wife a simple Patharenic peasant-serf girl. But when he ascended to the throne, he converted, in great pomp, back to Catholicism and discarded his poor peasant wife for a more suitable girl, a high born one. She was Katarina the daughter of the Duke of Hum (Herzegovina) who likewise was a Patharen. She also converted, became an ardent Catholic and after the conquest of Bosnia by the Turks, died in exile in Rome in great sanctity. Meanwhile, Stephen Thomas, himself, as a king became the greatest enemy of his former Patharenic-Good Christian co-religionists. Eventually, in 1459, he expelled from Bosnia all Good Christians who refused to recognize themselves as Catholics. After this and the Turkish conquest which followed soon (in 1463), the Good Christians went into rapid decline and disappeared shortly after. When Columbus discovered America in 1492, almost all Good Christians had either rejoined the Catholic church or had converted to Islam.

51. "trato y conversacion he tenido con gentes sabias, eclesiasticas y seglares, latinos y griegos, judios y moros y con otros muchos de otras sectas"—Bartolome de Las Casas—Op. Cit. vol. I, p. 31.

52. Dominik Mandić—Op. Cit. p. 69, note 220.

53. Ibid. p. 69, note 221.

54. Ibid. p. 69, note 222.

55. Dominik Mandić—MOSTAR U HERCEGOVINI, in "Hrvatski Kalendar", Chicago 1968, p. 100.
56. Juan de Torquemada—LIBELLUS SIUE TRACTATUS CONTRA ERRORES MANICHEORUM (1461), edit. D. Kamber—Kardinal Torquemada i tri Bosanska Bogomila", in "Croatia Sacra" III, Zagreb 1932.
57. Dominik Mandić—ETNIČKA POVIJEST BOSNE I HERCEGOVINE (Bosna i Hercegovina vol. III), Rome 1965, p. 49–50.
58. Alexandre V. Soloviev—LE TESTAMENT DU GOST RADIN, "Mandićev Zbornik" (Collectanea Mandić), Rome 1965, p. 151.
59. Ibid. p. 147.
60. Dominik Mandić—BOGOMILSKA CRKVA BOSANSKIH KRSTJANA (Bosna i Hercegovina vol. II), Chicago 1962, pp. 332–333, notes 39–43, p. 411, note 103.
61. "E le mando que haya encomendada a Beatriz Enriquez, madre de D. Fernando, mi hijo, que la provea que pueda vivir honestamente, como persona a quien yo soy en tanto cargo. Y eso se haga por mi descargo de conciencia, porque esto pesa mucho para mi anima. La razon de ello non es licito de la escribir aqui.—LOS QUATRO VIAJES DEL ALMIRANTE . . . p. 220.
62. See here page 109, Note 43.
63. Dominik Mandić—ETNIČKA POVIJEST BOSNE I HERCEGOVINE, vol. III, Rome 1967, pp. 136, 534–535.
64. Morison believes it means: "Servant I am of the Most High Saviour Christ the son of Mary" in which the initials "X" and "Y" stand for the words "Christ" and "son" in Greek language.—See: Samuel E. Morison—CHRISTOPHER COLUMBUS, MARINER, New York 1955, p. 64.
However, that the "X" and "Y" stand for "Christ" and "son" in Greek sounds rather fantastic for it implies also among other things that the woolweaver from Genoa knew even one such language as Greek!
65. COLUMBUS "UNMASKED" AS PORTUGAL'S MASTER SPY—Financial Times, London July 5, 1988, p. 3.
66. Ibid. p. 3.
67. Ibid. p. 3.
68. Ibid. p. 3.
69. Ibid. p. 3.
70. See here Part I, pp. 1–27.
71. In Columbus' time Dalmatia was literally inundated by nobility which had no possessions whatsoever. They were the nobles who fled the unceasing civil and religious strife. Members of this no-

bility supported themselves with "their swords" that is by enter-
ing into service of Venice, Spain, Free Croatia, later Hapsburg's
Austria and Germany, Hungary and other Western countries.
From the 15th to the 18th century this was the usual thing to do
in Dalmatia. This explains why Columbus and his brothers had
no possessions whatsoever in any one country. It must be pointed
out that those Colombos found in some Genoese papers were not
poor at all. They were rather moderately wealthy by the standards
of those times. Among other things they owned several buildings
in Genoa, and also a tavern in Savonna. Yet, we know that Christopher Columbus and his brothers not only never went to Genoa
but never inherited anything in Genoa and never made any legal
deed about the disposition of their property in Genoa.

72. FINANCIAL TIMES, London July 5, 1988, p. 3.—See note 65.

73. See here pages 42–43, also, Salvador de Madariage—CHRISTOPHER
    COLUMBUS, F. Ungar publ., New York 1967, pp. 127–128.

74. Ibid. pp. 127–128.

75. Ibid. pp. 127–128.

76. See here pp. 88–90.

77. See here p. 119.

78. See here pages 107–111.

79. Francis Dvornik—THE MAKING OF CENTRAL AND EASTERN
    EUROPE, London 1948, pp. 268–304.

80. Constantine VII, Porphyrogenitus—DE ADMINISTRANDO IM-
    PERIO, Constantinople, circa 950, ed. Moravcsik-Jenkins, Buda-
    pest 1949, p. 146. Dominik Mandić—RASPRAVE I PRILOZI, Rome
    1963, p. 55, cit.

81. Ibid. See Dominik Mandić—RASPRAVE I PRILOZI, Rome 1963,
    pp. 54–55.

82. Ibid. p. 54.

83. SUPETARSKI KARTULAR, No. 100, ed. V. Novak—P. Skok, Za-
    greb 1952, p. 230.

84. Dominik Mandić BOGOMILSKA CRKVA BOSANSKIH
    KRSTJANA, Chicago 1962, p. 343.

85. Ibid. p. 343.

86. Ibid. p. 343.

87. Ibid. p. 343.

88. Ibid. pp. 342–343.

89. Ibid. pp. 343–344.

90. "El cual mayorazgo en ninguna manera lo herede mujer ninguna,
    salvo si aqui ni en otro cabo del mundo no se fallase hombre de
    mi linaje verdadero que se hobiese llamado y llamase el y sus

antecesores de Colon" . . . —LOS CUATRO VIAJES DEL AL-
MIRANTE . . . pp. 217–218.

91. Dominik Mandić—ETNIČKA POVIJEST BOSNE I HERCEGO-
VINE, Rome 1967, p. 32, note 53.

92. Ibid. p. 32.

93. LOS CUATRO VIAJES DEL ALMIRANTE . . . pp. 217–218.

94. Samuel E. Morison—THE EUROPEAN DISCOVERY OF AMER-
ICA, The Northern Voyages A.D. 500–1600, Oxford Univ. Press,
New York 1971, p. 158.

95. In Dalmatia and everywhere along the Croatian Adriatic coast the
popular character of "barba Zvane" (Uncle Zvane), depicts a simple but wise good-natured and funny oldtimer.

96. Mario Caboga—"Satira dell'Arcidiacono Mario Caboga Gentil-
uomo Raguseo detto Cordiza et confuso contra la nobilita di Ragusi
e due suoi Sonetti contra la Dalmazia". Two transcripts of this
work are found in the Library of Little Brothers in Dubrovnik.
This Mario Caboga, who died in Rome in 1582, was the Arch-
deacon and general vicar of the Archdiocese of Dubrovnik.

97. DUBROVČANIN KABOGA I DUKA OD MLETAKA—Croatian
folk tale.

98. THE JOURNAL OF CHRISTOPHER COLUMBUS and the documents relating to the voyages of John Cabot and Gaspar Corte
Real—B. Franklin publ., New York (no year) pp. 217–219, 224–225.

99. Ibid. p. 218.

100. See here pages 64–65, 68.

101. Clements R. Markham—introduction to THE JOURNAL OF
CHRISTOPHER COLUMBUS and . . . p. XXI, (See here note 98).

102. Samuel E. Morison—Op. Cit. p. 625.

103. "Interesting Facts from the History of the Croatians in the United
States"—DIAMOND JUBILEE, Special edition of St. Cyril and
Methodius Parish, New York 1988.

104. Ibidem

105. Ibidem

106. HANDBOOK OF AMERICAN INDIANS North of Mexico—Edited
by Frederick Webb Hodge, New York 1959, p. 365.

107. THE JOURNAL OF CHRISTOPHER COLUMBUS and the documents relating to the voyages of John Cabot and Gaspar Corte
Real, B. Franklin publ. New York (no year)—Clements R. Markham in the introduction, p. XXI.

108. See here pages 81–85.

109. Salvador de Madariaga—Op. Cit. p. 364.

110. Ibid. p. 175.

111. If this does not constitute a proof that Christopher Columbus and his brothers were not Genoese I do not know what else would constitute a proof. If they were plain Genoese there is not one reason in this world why the sovereigns of Spain would steadfastly refuse to mention them as such. Certainly, the king and queen of Spain, Ferdinand and Isabella, knew the identity and national origin of their Admiral as well as the real truth about the origin of the discovery of the New World. That information was, undoubtedly, divulged to them, under the oath of secrecy by Columbus himself in 1492. That's why he never figures in royal papers as a Genoese-Italian.

112. Salvador de Madariaga—Op. Cit. pp. 175–176.

113. Antonio Ballesteros y Beretta—CRISTOBAL COLON Y EL DESCUBRIMIENTO DE AMERICA, Barcelona 1945, p. 678.

114. Ibid. pp. 678, 680.

115. Ibid. p. 679.

116. Everything of the little what we know about Fray Gaspar Gorricio points out toward his Croatian origin. Here it is interesting to add one further note: Gorricio's booklet "Contemplations over a Rosary" was published in Seville in 1495, by two foreign printers, Meynart Ungut and Lancalao Polono, of which the latter, Lancalao Polono (Polonić) has a Croatian name. This may have been the reason why they were the ones who printed Gorricio's work. This Croatian name, Polonić, also comes in its Italianized form—Polonio—and there are still numerous Polonios in Croatia today. One Polonić family is particularly known in Dubrovnik and, Southern Dalmatia the region from which most probably both, Columbus and Cabot also came. On the roster of sea captains in Dubrovnik between the years 1626-1636, the name Polonić is listed. (so is that of Polo).

117. In conclusion it should be added that even the physical description we have of Columbus correspondes to a Croatian type, particularly the contemporary one. Reddish hair, blue eyes, and aquiline nose are the traits closely associated with that what is scientifically classified as the Dinarian type of man (from Dinara, a mountain in Southern Croatia).

A study of Columbus' character also reveals a typical Croatian. His quickness of temper, certain boastfulness and constant habit of complaining are not entirely strange to a Croatian character, but most of all, the tenacity with which he stuck to the convictions once acquired, that is to say his notorious hardheadedness is an especially striking trait of the Croatian character, particularly the Southern one.

Neither is his extraordinary career that strange for a Croatian of those times or for that matter of any time, before or after. He was a typical product of this adventurous spirit of the Croats, especially the Dalmatian ones, who seemingly "specialized" in producing the colorful, fantastic and sometime controversial personages whose combined traits Christopher Columbus exhibited. He was an aristocrat and a beggar, pirate and admiral, imitator but also explorer on his own imbued with boundless fantasy, a crusader and also a religious reformer of a sort, writer and adventurer with a touch of an impostor, but a genial one. Yes, Croatians have produced many folks like that beginning with Marco Polo, his procursor and idol, who did not mind letting his fantasy work, exaggerating a little and more than a little. And that other Croat and his contemporary, John Cabot, was exactly the same. He was almost his replica. Similar was another of his Croatian contemporaries, Andrija Zamometić, called Zuccalmaglio, the noted church rebel from Nin who convoked the Council in Basel and tried to reform the Catholic church and dethrone Pope Sixtus IV. Similar also was, later, Pavao (Paul) Skalić the self-proclaimed "Prince of Skala and Hum" who made believers in half of Europe and ended-up as a Prime Minister of Prussia. Similar was another Dalmatian Croat, Count Stephen Zanović, a man of letters and also in his time the rival of the then aging Casanova in Venice and self-proclaimed descendant of Skanderbeg, the "Prince of Albania" and pretender to the trone of Albania whose adventures almost provoked a war between Venice and Holland. Similar was another one, that like Columbus was an anonymous Dalmatian Croat from the islands, who went into the mountainous country of Montenegro in the Turkish Empire with a brilliant idea and convinced the simple mountaineers that he was, in reality, the Russian czar Peter III, whom his wicked wife Catharine did not succeed in killing. He also convinced them that they should make him their ruler, which they did. He proclaimed himself an emperor (surnamed "Little czar Stephen") and led the successful resistance of the Montenegrins against the Ottoman Empire for several years until he was, by treachery, captured and killed by the Turks.

Christopher Columbus, no less successful talker and boastful person, according to all indications, seems to have been cut from that same material.